MANAGER'S
DIARY

A Handbook for
First Generation Entrepreneurs

MANAGER'S DIARY

A Handbook for
First Generation Entrepreneurs

UMESH DASHRATHI

PARTRIDGE
A Penguin Random House Company

To order additional copies of this book, contact
Partridge India
000 800 10062 62
orders.india@partridgepublishing.com

www.partridgepublishing.com/india

Dedicated to

Hon'ble Shri Narendra Modi
Prime Minister of India
Sir, none other than you understands importance
of entrepreneurs in the progress of the nation.

ACKNOWLEDGEMENT

I must mention that I am not a trained or professional writer. The book is an outcome of encouragement from my numerous friends and family members. Mentioning few names will be an injustice with the un-named. I am thankful to all of them who helped me directly and indirectly.

I started, grown and sustained business till now, only due to some timely motivating remarks of my late father, Mr. Martandrao Y. Dashrathi. I would like to be indebted to him forever. My mother, late Mrs. Shakuntala is always a source of inspiration.

My wife Dr. Jyoti categorically encouraged me for this book. Son Rohit and daughter Rucha are the first readers and critics. Their contribution is invaluable.

Sincere thanks to Penguin / Partridge team for all their support and patience.

Umesh Dashrathi

Long Story of a Short Book

One fine morning in March 2012, I received a call. On the other end was Mr. Sanjay Lodha, a good friend now, requesting me to come to Nasik, Maharashtra for delivering a lecture on "Building Sustainable Enterprise" in the month of April. I wondered on couple of things. Who referred my name and can I really deliver something on this topic? Subsequently, my first doubt was resolved. I received a call from Mr. Harish Baijal, a senior cop officer, earlier in Aurangabad, my home town and the then in Nasik, requesting for the same event. Answer to the second question was possible only after the event.

With somewhat hesitation and dilemma, I accepted the invite, prepared a 35 slide power point presentation, went to Nasik on 22nd April 2012 morning, delivered the lecture and came back by afternoon to Aurangabad. The speech was woven around Building Sustainable Enterprise by First Generation Entrepreneur. The presentation was very simple. Minimum one or maximum three words on each slide, supported by quotable quote on the bottom. The whole speech was only evaluation of personal experience and observing other colleagues, thru eyes of first generation entrepreneur.

The feedback was very good. Everyone appreciated. Many unknown people categorically phoned me.

There were number of friend requests on Linkedin. Ms. Sonia, from the audience got connected. Till date I am playing a role of her elder brother and adviser.

Again in Feb 2013, I was invited by the same forum, as a special invitee. This time no lecture, but as I went there, many people greeted me for last year's lecture. To my surprise, many of them were telling the points, as it is, with many details, in my speech. This was amazing! I personally never came across any speaker whom I could recollect with each point. I was stunned and praising memory of those people who could remember many of my points, as they were! Still, I was curious, how so many people can have sharp memory and could recollect the same content at a time? Being data finicky, my conclusion was simple : People from Nasik, Maharashtra are sharp and intelligent!!!!!!!

In May 2013, I received a call from a respected senior friend, philosopher and guide, Mr. CP Tripathi. He is the Founder President of Aurangabad Management Association. (AMA). AMA started a series of lectures viz. "Rare Share". There were number of dignitaries who graced the event. It was an honour for me. Also, the call being from Mr CP Tripathi in person, there was no question of denial. Being little enthused with earlier theme, I woven my "Rare Share" in similar format. The whole speech was only analysis, personal thoughts and observations about other first generation colleagues, thru eyes of first generation entrepreneur. No management jargons, no hi-fi statements, no data obsession!

This time almost 80% audience knew me. Many of them were familiar to me since my childhood. It was a difficult task to share the rare in front of the audience who knew you inside out! My journey was an open book for all of them. I delivered the lecture with lot of butterflies in stomach. It was @ 35 minutes of stressed session followed by 40 minutes of QA. Over! I never had a sigh of relief this before! To my great surprise, again a lot of appreciation! Mr. Ram Bhogale, one of my most respected senior friends, an authority in Maharashtra Industrial circle, notable industrialist, invited me to his industry for interaction with his senior team. With same intention, many others also approached.

I was again astonished when some of them started telling me the points I referred in the speech, in details. Are the people in Aurangabad also equally brilliant as Nasik? (Being native of Aurangabad, I knew the fact! ;)). It was something different.

On elaborative analysis, I realised that the points I was referring in my lecture, were more or less experienced by every first generation entrepreneur. There was a direct connect on every event. The people talking to me were correlating their experiences with whatever I was telling. That was the reason they were perfectly reproducing my thoughts.

Discussing with many other colleagues in industry and business, I realised that every first generation entrepreneur is passing thru almost same cycle. The problems are similar, hence solutions are similar.

Going further, I found the same sequence of experiences for professionals. And here a new but realistic definition of an Entrepreneur was born. Entrepreneur is not a synonym for Businessman. **Entrepreneur is one who outperforms!** First Generation Entrepreneur is someone who outperforms in the family. He can be a professional, a businessman, an employee or anyone, who crossed the boundaries to go to the next level.

In the meantime of two Nasik visits, I was also called by some educational institutes like VIT Pune, SCMLRD Pune, GECA Aurangabad and some more. I interacted the enthuse students and was excited by realising their urge. They were young, intelligent and curious. There questions were very innocent and basic. In one of the lectures, one young student asked, "I want to do something. What should I do?" I had no answer at that point. I was restless with that question. It was the same question, I asked to someone, before 25 years!!!!!!!!!!!!

With that question, my agitation increased day by day. I started reminiscing my struggling days. Suddenly I recollected; strong desire of doing "something" is like an unguided missile. I was also striking aimlessly on number of doors, resulting in breaking my head several times. Now my eyes were always seeing "that" student with a fire in the belly, running around to find "something". Was I seeing myself again?

In my struggling days, lot of decisions I took, went absolutely wrong. I could have ruined myself with those decisions. I was fortunate to get some "Guru" at the important stages of life. Someone or other guided me or helped me to overcome the situation.

This was the birth point of this book. After some sleepless nights I decided to reply to "that" gentleman, who was "me", few years back. I was sure there must be number of budding entrepreneurs, trying to find this answer. I said to myself, "Let me try if I can help them!" Thus, here I am, making an attempt to do so by reaching them with this book.

The book is not only about my personal experiences. It is more of a collection of thoughts from my own experience, experience of my fellow colleagues who are much better entrepreneurs than me and my observations of surrounding atmosphere.

The beneficiaries from this book can be First generation entrepreneurs (FGEs), Professionals, Employees in senior position, Budding Entrepreneurs and Students who want to do "Something".

Just for understanding, the book is divided in three parts:

➤ Starting of Business
➤ Growth of Business
➤ Sustaining the Business

For further simplicity, every part is divided in three subparts:

✓ Personal
✓ Internal
✓ External

At the end, there is a consolidated matrix of all points discussed in the book for better understanding and ease. Based on individual perceptions, the points may ponder from one section to other without affecting the context.

The whole book is based on KISS principle, Keep It Straight and Simple! There is no management terminology, no data mania and no influence of management lingo. This is a simple and individual analysis of a life of a first generation entrepreneur. Though personal, I found it is applicable to everyone who is trying to outperform.

Me being from industry, an industrial environment prevails number of times. It is my humble request to view this from your own environment or replace "industry" with your profession. I am sure you will find an instant connection.

INDEX

3. Sustenance

START

Personal

MONEY

Problems are not stop signs, they are guidelines.
Robert H Schuler

"How to raise funds for business?"
"Business is possible only if one
has spare funds with him."
"Business is monopoly of XXX community."
"Business is not our cup of tea."
"Business has to be in genes."

These are some commonly heard comments in any typical family, where a youngster wants to do business. Rather, it is firmly believed that someone who does not have spare money with him cannot do the business. If this is true, just look at following examples:

- ✓ A son of primary school teacher in a small village created an empire called Reliance and became a brand called Dhirubhai Ambani.
- ✓ A college dropout son of a lawyer father and teacher mother is today known as Bill Gates.
- ✓ A person struggled for survival from childhood, thrown away from company created by him, created an iconic brand called Apple. We call him Steve Jobs.
- ✓ A husband borrowed ₹ 10000/- (USD 200/-) from his wife to start the business. He is an IT idol today. World calls him Narayanmurthy.

- ✓ Twins of a shoe factory supervisor, who lost his job and everything in the great recession, created McDonalds.
- ✓ An unqualified fourth class pass out person starts making chocolates, Milton Hershey. Hershey is the largest selling brand today.

If money is everything, why did all these individuals could succeed? All of them were with an average mediocre economic background. None of their parents had huge bank balance to offer the kin. Then what was that X factor, making these people to enter in Forbes list? How did their organisations enter in Fortune 500 Companies? Difficult questions!!!!!!

Answer to these questions may give some lead to understand the process of becoming entrepreneur. Let us try to understand the trigger points of these gentlemen, in the same sequence:

- ➤ Dhirubhai Ambani was highly passionate to do business.
- ➤ Bill Gates was crazy for IT and persuaded IBM to install his software.
- ➤ Steve Jobs was a creative soul.
- ➤ Narayanmurthy was abused badly by his superior.
- ➤ For McDonald Bros., earning money was a dire need, as the father lost his job.
- ➤ For Milton Hershey, family survival was a big issue.

Answer to all complex problems is always simple. See if following steps make sense.

- Discover your passion. (Dhirubhai Ambani and Bill Gates
- Identify your skills. (Steve Jobs and Narayanmurthy)
- Know what you are best at. (McDonalds and Milton Hershey).
- And adopt it as your business!

On rational grounds, the ideas may sound foolish. Let it be! People may laugh at your brain child. Let them laugh! Pursue your interests. They will guide you the treasure. They will show the ways and means to raise the funds.

There are many examples which prove that money is not everything. The needs are attitude, passion and creative ideas. Passion comes through self commitment. Attitude is in born. Creative ideas are free of cost. Money comes thru ideas.

Starting with what you like, makes the job interesting. You can give your best. Money follows. You start discovering ideas which will make money.

In this journey, it is not necessary that success will meet you on the nearest station. It can be at much longer distance than you predict. May be you will change the track in between. Doesn't matter. Your wholehearted efforts and passion will guide you correctly. There could be some problem on the way. Not to worry. Scarcity of money is obvious. Only precious things are scarce. Just open yourself. Every treasure needs a hunt. Keep trying.

Check with yourself, if "I don't have money" is an excuse your subconscious mind is giving to your conscious mind. Is it a face saving for not doing anything? Have you defined the exact problem? Do you know exactly how much money you need? Had you ever tried with bankers? Are you aware of all options of raising funds? Anytime you discussed your ideas with Private Equity Fund guys or Venture Capital personnel?

I am sure, if you are facing problem in raising funds, you have not tried many of the above things.

Most important to remember, raising money should always be with legal and ethical means. This will channelize your mind in right direction and avoid undue pressures.

(N.B. : No one in the world knows the answer of "How to raise money?" and if someone knows, he will never share it with anybody. ☺)

CLARITY OF THOUGHTS

<u>Begin with the end in mind</u>

A budding entrepreneur is always in the state of confusion. He has strong desires but no concrete plans. He is restless and tries on all possible options.

As mentioned in earlier chapter, during starting phase of business, one has to identify his core competence and work around the same. He has to analyse, in given circumstances and limitations, what best he can do.

Rigorous planning will lead to move upward on ladder of success. Failing to plan is planning to fail. Your planning may fail; still it will teach you a new useful lesson. In his famous quote on number of failures during invention of electric bulb, Thomas Alva Edison "I have not failed. I've just found 1,000 ways that won't work." His goal was clear. He wanted to convert electrical energy into light. Despite of lot of failures, he never lost his focus. As a result, he not only lighted the world but delighted the universe.

Identification of goal is one of the most important things to start. Once that is done, half of the battle is won. With setting the goal, path is automatically visible. The real problem is how to identify or fix the goal? There are three most popular methods of finding your goals.

1) Finding what you know the best
2) Finding goal thru pleasure
3) Finding goal thru trouble

Let us elaborate all of them.

1) Finding what you know the best :

You can rely on your experience. You might have worked in some area as an employee or voluntarily. You know the ins and outs of that job. Business can best happen if you work in your core competence. Personally, I started a service station for two wheelers, as a beginning of my business carrier. This was not because I liked it the most but only because I knew it the most. Due to my earlier assignment, I knew about two wheelers, inside out. It was my core competence. In India, in those days, this was supposed to be a mediocre business. In a way, I was too qualified to do such a lower end business. However, that was the only business in which I could perform. I opted for it and subsequently after establishing, diversified to other areas for phenomenal growth.

2) Finding goal thru pleasure:

What do you like? C'mon, you know Sachin Tendulkar loves batting. If you love cooking, open a restaurant. Ask yourself what you like to do the most.

From above like list, analyze what business has topmost potential and start the same. Somebody famously said, if you are born Indian, forget soccer and play cricket. Opportunists! (I only said it ;-))

I will give you a live example of finding goals from pleasure.

In Mumbai, India, lives a young guy, Sandeep Gajakas, 28 years old. He was fanatic, almost obsessed about cleanliness. He wanted everything clean and bright, his house, his phone, his spectacles, his shoes, everything! This liking of cleanliness proved to be a great business for him. He thought of the requirement of cleanliness in ascending order. First in the list was footwear. The market was huge wrapping almost the whole population of India. He started his first "Shoe Laundry" in Mumbai. Having 7 franchises across India and continues to receive hundred of enquiries for more.

3) Finding goal thru trouble:

Find out what troubles you most. Work out the ways which will remove these troubles. May be others are facing same troubles. See if this can be your market. Start your business in this potential market.

Here is another live example. Mr. Hanumant Gaikwad, hailing from Satara, Maharashtra India was working as a trainee engineer with Tata Motors Ltd., Pune India. He observed the trouble of housekeeping of the huge facility. He adopted this idea as a business. Today, apart from all national and multinational companies, he is also engaged for Rashtrpati Bhavan, residence of The President of India. A young guy in early 40's, employs 25000 employees, in his organisation "Bharat Vikas Group."

Start with goal in mind. Once you reach the same, identify new one. If the goal is too big, break it into smaller goals, just like what we do while eating a bread. Freezing on goal will give you the direction.

Clarity of thoughts helps in focussing on the goals. This avoids distraction. In this beginning phase, lot of attractions of opting various options may prevail, resulting in diversion from goals. If one is clear on "to do" list, it helps achieving desired results.

FAMILY SUPPORT

Home is where the heart is….

Your close nears and dears have a great influence on your life. A word of appreciation, an affectionate look, warm pat or jadoo ki zappi (lukewarm hug) has a potency to change the life of young entrepreneur.

A young and budding first generation entrepreneur is mystified. He needs psychological support. He needs someone who says "Don't worry. In good or bad, we are with you." These should necessarily be the close and intimate family members.

In and around, we find n number of examples who are on the top of the world due to support of the family. The reverse is also equally true. A small discouragement from the family may lead to devastate the urge to augment.

When he was in standard IVth, he was considered as an obtuse student. His mother supported him and started teaching him at home. World today says that he is the most intelligent human being, born on the universe till date, Albert Einstein! This is the power of family support.

One of the Great Kings in Indian History, King Shivaji, was sculptured by his mother Rajmata Jijabai. Barak Obama openly admits the share of Michelle Obama in his being President of USA.

I personally experienced this. It was the turning point of my life. I was working with a giant Indian automotive company, Bajaj Auto Limited. It was an attractive job for social status. The remuneration was excellent. A Lot of opportunities for growth were waving hands. Being from an average middle class family and the only, late born, pampered child in the family, there was a resistance for entering into business. My father was deadly against it.

He was a firm believer of the then trend of assuming the government job to be safest as it was pensionable. Hence, he wanted me to settle in some secured job.

Like all youngsters in the age group of 25-30, I was a rebellion. Despite of all resistance, one fine day, I resigned from my job to do "something(?)". For more than a fortnight, my parents did not know my move. After they realised that I quit my job, the home environment was stunned and furious. Everyone almost stopped talking to me. I was side-lined by the family!

It did not take me more than couple of months to realise the harsh reality of the crooked world. There was no concrete plan. It was funny how the so called "business commitments" by someone were now termed as "casual discussions". The selling price expected by customer was not covering raw material cost also. A friend who offered that business, turned to be a customer now. There was a sudden change in the language. It was much more professional than informal. (I realised in next 25 years, this is how it happens everywhere, every time.)

I was frustrated. Depression was prevailing. Suddenly from a prestigious job, I was unemployed. The total family was dependent on me. I already hurt them. Why would they support me? And even if they desire to help, in what way? Father was retired from service. We were a typical average middle class Indian family, hoping on the only child, who left the job "happily"!

Those few days were the most difficult days in my life.

Probably, my father sensed my unrest. He came to me, hold my hand and patted! It was a divine pat. It was a shower of blessings. He said, "Do not worry. We are with you. Rest assured, family will not have a problem of two meals a day till I am alive."

It was not my father, but my destiny patting me and talking to me. These sentences turned my life upside down. It was my reincarnation. Fortunately, throughout his life time, I never used his single penny for running the family. But this was only due to his encouragement in the difficult time. Today I am doing a sizeable business, made possible only by those three lines said by my father. This is the power the family has!

FIRE IN THE BELLY

Always bear in mind that your own resolution to succeed is more important than any one thing
Abraham Lincoln

A first generation entrepreneur is entering in an unknown region. He is paving untrodden path. He faces lot of hurdles. His success is directly proportional to his determination.

Abraham Lincoln lost almost every election, also could not do well in any walk of his career. His law practice was mediocre. But when he won the first election to be a Senator, he straightway laddered to be the most beloved President of USA, which he is till this date.

No war can be won without fortitude. Napoleon could conquer the world because his dictionary did not have the word "impossible". Walt Disney was eldest amongst the five children of Elias Disney, his father. Elias was a farmer and unsuccessful businessmen. Success of Walter to become Walt Disney lies in his famous quote "It is kind of fun to do impossible". He converted a small idea of cartoon making into a very big industry. Now, animation industry is a separate sector.

A sincere desire brings out the best. If one has a strong will to do something, one will cross all the limiting boundaries. One will find opportunities to achieve the goal and if he could not find one, he will create it! He sleeps, wakes, dines, drinks with the idea. For the period, the concept or idea becomes his life. He won't be able to think beyond the goal. Both, right and left brains start working with supernatural speed.

Fire in the belly can be best illustrated with an example of a genuine Romeo. We see them everywhere. (May be we are one of them sometime☺). When someone is in love, he will do anything and everything for his beloved. He waits on her regular route for hours, does bike stunts to impress, collect all possible information and what not. The strong affection, in other words, fire in the belly will make him do all those acts. And if the attempts are genuine, intents are right and method is correct, there are bright chances of success. Unfortunately, the same Romeo, when it comes to work, gets pressurised and runs away from the task. What can be the better paradox? The same person wins in love and fails on business! He had already experienced the fruits of fire in the belly. He knows the importance of passion. He gives his best for love and succeeds, whereas does not give his best for other task and fails.

In the Start phase, fire in the belly is the essential parameter. If one does not feel this, he should think ten times to enter into the venture. Otherwise it will be nothing but the waste of time.

Presence of fire in the belly shows clear symptoms. Just check with yourself that how many times you catch yourself with following thoughts?

- Resentment
- Insomnia
- Continuous irritation
- Feeling of "Life is Boring"

- Feeling of Frustration
- Feeling of Depression

If you have all or some of the symptoms, surely you have some fire in you. Wake up, identify the same and start working on it!

POSITIVE THINKING

Whether you think you can, or you
think you can't, you are right.
Henry Ford

"I am not getting business because the concerned
officer does undue favour to other party"
"Boss favours her on gender basis"
"In this company, only relatives are preferred."
"Only racism, you know."

Surely, all of us are coming across such whispers. Such
thoughts often come out of desperation. Remember
the circumstances when you whispered this last. It is
normally when you have lost some order / promotion
/ assignment. In the same situation, if you have won
the same order / promotion / assignment, you would
have praised yourself.

Such thoughts are normally biased, moreover
negative. They come out as one is in denial mode.
He/she is not courageous to face the reality. The after
effects of such thoughts lead in losing the battle before
entering the battlefield. The only remedy is positive
thinking.

Positive thinking is most commonly used term. If
practiced, it yields wonderfully. It will boost energy
from within.

We can complain because rose bushes have thorns,
or rejoice because thorn bushes have roses.

Action creates success. Inaction creates nothing.

Mahatma Gandhi, all time Indian legend said, "Keep your thoughts positive because your thoughts become your words. Keep your words positive because your words become your behaviour. Keep your behaviour positive because your behaviour becomes your habit. Keep your habits positive because your habits become your values. Keep your values positive because your values become your destiny."

Positive thinking will always lead to cool mind. It will spread cheer in the environment.

King Porus was a war prisoner of Alexander the Great. When Alexander the Great asked how he should be treated, he answered, "As one King treats other". Alexander would have easily killed him. But he liberated King Porus. This was to add a friend than a foe. Alexander was thinking positive and finished one enemy. If he would have thought negative and killed Porus, the followers of Porus would have been his permanent enemies.

Negativity creates pressures. It is a path towards depression. Disasters are brood of negativity. Against, positivity will reduce pressures. It helps you to open your mind. Open mind performs hundred times better. Positivity enhances motivation. Motivated souls only can be passionate.

In the history of modern world, the most powerful example of positive thinking is struggle of India for freedom. In any freedom struggle across the Globe, the only way used was to unionise and retaliate with arms and ammunition. Terrorism is replied by terrorism. After lot of blood shedding, fittest would survive! Nothing different than jungle raj. Against this traditional heritage, in India, "Non Violence" and "Civil Disobedience" were the tools used successfully. Probably, this is the one of its kind, in the history of mankind. British Government was forced to leave India, without shedding a drop of blood. This is the strength of positive thinking.

In my industrial life, when I was in the start phase of my career, there was an opportunity. I was offered a big ticket business by my customer. The offer was equivalent to 10 multiples of the then existing annual turnover. It was a great opportunity but asking for huge investment, I never thought of. If I would have succeeded, my growth in two years would have been 10 times! The flip side was, the investments needed were 3 times of my present annual revenue! So, if I lose, I will go bankrupt!!!!!!!!!!

I decided to en-cash the opportunity. Thought process was very simple. One, such opportunities do not knock every day. Second, the required core competence is available with me. What is not available is money, which bankers are providing. Third, if I fail, then what? Answer was, if I want different results than what I am getting today, I need to do something different. Fourth, if I do not try, I am already failed. Better try and fail.

I faced the challenge and succeeded! Positive thinking.

KNOW THOU & BE COURAGEOUS

"It is hard to fail, but it is worse never to have tried to succeed."
Theodore Roosevelt

"What will happen I do not succeed?"
"People will laugh at me."
"My relatives will keep distance from my family."
"Will father like this?"

First generation entrepreneur will always have such dilemma. Nothing wrong! His social and family background will pull him back. Fear of the unknown always prevails. It is relatively simple to think out of the box. Difficult part is execution.

You need lot of courage to overcome this psyche. Remember, success will run behind the people who work tirelessly. It is a slave of those who believe in themselves.

Here is a story of a legendary man, the second Minister of Finance of independent India, Mr. C.D. Deshmukh. In his early days, after completion of University education, he appeared for Civil Services Exams. The day results declared, his friend rushed to find him. After spotting him on a regular badminton court, with sheer excitement, he told Mr. Deshmukh that results are out. The cool question from other side was "Oh! Who is the rank second?"

See the amazing confidence!

Human being is an amazing creation of nature. Everyone is unique. There is no duplication. Even twins are not similar. Everyone is intellectual. Many times we misrepresent the intellect with academic qualification. It can be in anything. There is no limit to intelligence. It is not a monopoly of any class. There is no correlation of intelligence and academic career.

There are seven categories of intelligence.

> Spatial (Artistic)
> Kinesthetic Intelligence (Athletes / Players))
> Musical Intelligence (Musicians)
> Linguistic Intelligence (Writers)
> Logical / Mathematical Intelligence (IQ)
> Interpersonal Intelligence (Management)
> Intrapersonal Intelligence (Knows himself)

The scientific study revealed that every human being has all these intelligence, with different degree of strength. One with spatial intelligence may not have a good IQ, but he/she is excellent in art. Other may not be good in management but can do wonderful music compositions. Some one cannot write well but is the best athlete. Identify where you can fit and find opportunities in that area.

MS Dhoni could not complete his university studies, but he is the topmost cricketer in the world. Milton Hershey could not study beyond 4th standard, but he created brand named Hershey, largest selling chocolates in the world.

Believe that we are born for some purpose. We should not die like all other creatures. We should be remembered for "something". We have the most precious thing with us, our brain. Do not fill it with fear. If it is filled with fear, there will be no space for other thoughts.

A young person from Porbander goes to South Africa. He is thrown out of train for racism. With his self belief and fearless attitude, he could raise a non violence movement, creating history. Today we call him Mahatma (Great Soul) Gandhi.

In Montgomery, year 1955, Rosa Parks refused the order to give up her seat in the colour section to a passenger, after the section was filled. Others followed and this was the birth of "Civil Rights Movement" in America.

He, who cannot believe in himself, cannot believe in others too. He enters in inferiority complex, leading to consecutive failures. This is own creation. If you are in that phase and want to come out, start right now. Know yourself. Believe yourself. You can establish your world.

CREATIVITY

"You see things; and you say, 'Why?' But I dream things that never were; and I say, 'Why not'?"
George Bernard Shaw

As we defined earlier, entrepreneur is one who outperforms. Only creative people think to be an entrepreneur. If you are thinking to be an entrepreneur, you are creative.

Human species are rare in the universe. The most infallible power we possess is creativity. This creativity shows us the past and gives the vision of future. We are aware of the history million of years back. We know about the stars and planets billions of miles away from us. Still we could not find any other species like us. Even on earth, where life exists, there are no other species like us. The main difference is about creativity. Someone like us can create Mars Rover which runs untiringly, millions of miles away from us. To understand the birth of universe, Higgs Boson is artificially made. There are plans to colonise on Mars. Just today, when I am writing this, a space shuttle crossed our solar system to travel for infinity, still connected with signals.

Above examples indicate the creativity potential of mankind. We should be proud of being human.

An entrepreneur needs creativity. Especially first generation entrepreneur can use it as a tool. He needs to do something different from others. That is his foremost requirement. Otherwise he will extinct. Every one of us possesses creativity. It should be used generously. Generous use will multiply it ten times. Let the ideas flow. Only few will succeed. Normally, success rate is less than 5 percent. You do not know if this 5% is first or last. Keep on trying.

Probably, there cannot be a better example than Apple, on this earth. Surely, you understand this Apple not being the Adam's but Steve Jobs.

Bible tells that world is created due to an apple ate by Eve. Today Apple created another virtual world. You have everything you can imagine, in this Apple's virtual world. You can have pets, make friends, kill demons, worship gods, and compose music and so on! With Apple apps, you can do anything to stretch to your imagination. What a creativity! It is just an amazing idea of an individual. It is astonishing! Any word in dictionary is insignificant to describe this creativity.

Imagination is mother of creativity. Start imagining! Henry Ford imagined making tons of cars and methodology of mass production was created. Mr. Toyoda imagined perfection and Toyota Production System is born. Malasiya had thrown away one part for its unlawful activities and drug trafficking. Lee Kuan Yew, accepted the challenge and created a city. It is world's busiest port today and we call it Singapore.

Creativity has no racial limitation, no national boundary, no age constraint, no gender constriction and no status restriction.

The major enemies of creativity are
1) Stress
2) Complacency

Stressed mind cannot create ideas. Worry and stress if reside in brain or heart, occupies all space and do not leave any space for creativity. Be careful on both these vampires. They suck the blood thru neck. Kick them out. Replace them with creativity.

BE HUMBLE

*True humility is not thinking less of
yourself; it is thinking of yourself less
C.S. Lewis*

Ice cool head and sweetie tongue are typical identities of a successful entrepreneur. One can easily identify the entrepreneur watching these intrinsic worth.

This virtue is the most liked by any customer. One of the hidden agenda of any customer is to test humility of the supplier. This is tested not only by spoken words, but also by
- Pitch of voice
- Tone of voice
- Body language
- Good etiquettes / Mannerism
- Greeting styles
- Warm eye to eye contacts
- Listening habits

Most of the times, all above characteristics attack on subconscious mind of the other side. It may not be tangibly understood or spoken, but creates some uneasy feeler or otherwise. So to say; we also do not like somebody for no reason. We do not gel well with someone, without knowing why it is so? There is no enmity, no argument, no disagreement; still presence of someone unnecessarily bothers us. The cause lies in some of the above points.

An entrepreneur does not want to be disliked. Hence, he should always take care of his acts and deeds very carefully.

High pitch of voice indicates your hostile moods. Sharp and cutting voice indicates rebelling attitude. This is the most disliked. Modulate your pitch of voice.

Loud tone indicates dictating and dominating mind-set. Normally others will agree on the face but will not appreciate behind the back. Control your volume.

Body language never misrepresents. Your words may say anything; your eyes cannot talk untrue. Your posture will clearly indicate what is going on in your head. Your walking style tells your mood, so on and on. Master the body language. Numbers of good books on the subject are available.

Good etiquettes will always create a good impression. It tells about your background. Level of a person is mainly judged with etiquettes and mannerisms. Reading messages on cell phone when the other person is talking with us, or cleaning nose in a gathering of people are some bad mannerism examples. You can find many around.

There are examples of losing business due to bad mannerism. Take care to follow etiquettes and tag along mannerisms.

Greeting style makes first impression and first impression cannot be made second time. Greeting style clearly indicates your views about the other person. It is different for respected person than for a young boy than for a disliked person. It emerges automatically. You need not think on this. Simple handshake tells a lot about your views about the person. A firm hand shake indicates your confidence and liking about the other person. Cold handshake indicates you do not value the other fellow. Not looking in eyes and shaking hand reveals that you are under confident. There can be numerous pointers like this.

Incidentally, business calls for limiting certain dislikes to ourselves. Always greet cheerfully!

Eye to eye contact plays a vital role. Eyes are considered as reflection of mind. It tells whether you like the other person or not. It indicates annoyance or tenderness. It differentiates evil spirit from love and affection. One should be able to demonstrate the warmth through eyes.

Listening carefully is a sign of humbleness. One wants to talk than to listen. As a normal gesture, with little exaggeration, talking is considered as offending and listening as defending. Everyone likes offending. In confined limits, entrepreneur does what others want. He gives a chance to other person to do what he likes. He lets the other person talk. And he listens carefully taking interest in what others are saying. We can imagine the pleasure other person gets if he is heard patiently.

Humbleness is not synonymous to flattery. It is a sign of respect. It shows how much do you value the other person. It generates positive energy. It glitters the environment. Be humble and modest.

EMOTIONAL ATTACHMENT

Desire to sense objects comes from attachment to sense objects, and anger comes from unfulfilled desires.
Bhagavad Gita

During start of the business, one should be attached with it emotionally. This attachment is with reference to organisation. This brings in passion. The emotional attachment makes you day dreaming. It is like romancing with the beloved. When you think about your fiancée, you tend to forget everything else. It is the one and only one thought in your mind. You fully concentrate. A small probability of disengaging makes you restless and panic.

When you have affection and love for someone, you are ready to do anything and everything for him or her. You spend sleepless nights, travel hundreds of miles, think only about the person, stretch your limits, cross your boundaries, show off a bit to impress and get excited with a thought of cohabitation. One fine morning your dream comes true and your beloved is converted to your life partner. Adopt the same methodology and make your business as your fiancée, during starting phase of business.

Path for achieving what you want is always painful. Nobody likes to toil. But when you are in love or emotionally attached, exertion is not felt. Every small achievement is enjoyed. Every opportunity is en-cashed. Love does wonders. Romeo can die for

Juliet and Qaise happily accepts stoning for Laila. Be a Romeo and make your business as Juliet. Be ready to die for it.

Emotions are a precious gift of nature to human beings. There are great examples of what emotions can do. Emotions can turn down dynasties. It can make or break the organisations.

Passion is an outcome of emotional attachment. Only emotionally attached persons can be passionate.

When I started the business, in first six months, I had to face a severe labour unrest. The reason was not internal issues, but someone from outside was trying to create unrest for his own vested interests. I was indebted with huge bank loans, at least three times of my total revenues at that point. During the unrest, business came to standstill. I was in a fix. Customers were annoyed as I was unable to supply. Bankers were visiting frequently, making their own judgements and writing adverse reports. Government officers were sending notices, one after the other. Different labour unions were trying to take undue advantage. Local goons were taking an opportunity to add in the chaos. Competitors were enjoying.

If the issue is not resolved in minimum time, I smelt nothing less than bankruptcy. And the route to resolve was very simple. Surrender! A complete surrender and accepting the undue demands, nothing less than extortion, would have solved all problems immediately.

If I would not have emotionally attached with the business, surely it was the best and immediate solution. I was foreseeing the future problems in this solution. It would have been digging the own grave for tomorrow. As I was in the role of father of this newly born child, it was not possible to do that. I decided to fight! Zero tolerance was the policy. All ill elements were removed from the factory. Trouble makers were thrown out immediately. "No nonsense" was the message demonstrated loudly.

As I was on right footing morally and ethically, once I decided to fight, solutions started coming in. It took me one long year to eradicate the ill elements, but it happened. Today, after 15 years the same labours with us and practically enjoying the work. We are grown almost 20 times. If I would not have emotionally attached, probably the courageous decision would not be possible and today surely we were extinct.

(NB : The episode mentioned above was one of the extremely traumatic one. I must mention here that I was supported by number of genuine friends, selflessly, to come out of the situation. They were also emotionally attached with me. This underlines the importance of selfless friends in your life. Honestly, lion's share of my so called success goes to many of such friends, who were my friend, philosopher or guide at various modes of life. Nevertheless, family members, specially my better half, were boosting my morale all the time.)

EARLIER THE BETTER

I started my first business when I was 14 years old and it was too late to start.
Warren Buffet

Time is a unidirectional vector. It will only move forward, at least till the time machine is discovered in reality. One cannot go back in time and again become young. So start as early as possible, before you start growing old.

No two individuals have same resources. No one has same money, same property, same bank balance, same relations, same godfather, same rich and helping friends, etc….

The only same thing which two individuals share is 'time'.

There are only 24 hours in everyone's day and 365 days in a year. Everybody's minute clocks in 60 seconds and weeks finish in 7 days.

Time is the only resource, which is common to all human beings. It does not discriminate in rich and poor, king and beggar, businessman and employee, CEO and clerk, men and women. Then why only few people reach high altitudes and others not? You, I and Bill Gates have equal time. Then why Bill Gates only can conquer the world? Why he is managing world's largest enterprise successfully while you and I are stressed with our routine? Despite of running the largest economy of the world, Mr. Obama finds a break with his family and we are so busy in our routine that our family waits for years to go out for excursion. The simple answer is, those who utilise their time wisely, effectively and qualitatively, will grow and enjoy. Undoubtedly, there are other factors also for growth, but time management is the essential one. One, who wants to grow successfully, must manage his time effectively. So save your time. Start early, rather today… why not now?

It is always better to start earlier. Every new activity needs a learning cycle. Learning is always better and faster in younger age. Risk taking abilities are very high in tender age. The requirements are less. Family responsibilities and social commitments are limited. These are highly supporting factors for starting a new venture and entering in unknown environs.

Of course, this does not mean that age is a parameter for starting the business. There are number of success stories. Mr. Narayanmurthy started Infosys, when he was approaching 40s. Earlier also means as early as possible, the moment you start thinking. It is never too late and better late than never. As Mr. Benjamin Franklin famously said, "you may delay but time will not!"

START

Internal

FEAR FOR EXISTENCE

Do not let your fears choose your destiny.

Internal issues are nothing but the issues related to every stakeholder in the newly born organisation. The stakeholders are entrepreneur himself, his employees, suppliers and every related party. As the entrepreneur is affected the most, he has to demonstrate visibly on these issues. In the starting phase, "fear for existence" will always try to influence the decision making. Fear for existence can also be synonymous to "fear of unknown." This fear exists since ages. It is a trait of every human being. In our day to day life, we pray god to overcome this fear, we avoid cynical deeds to keep this fear away from our life.

In business, we avoid taking bold or radical steps as we are possessive of what we have. We fear to lose what is achieved till date. Resistance to change will try to predominate. Beware! This fear may control our destiny.

The best way to overcome the fear is to face it as early as possible. More delay means keeping the fear in mind for a longer time. When fear occupies your mind, it leaves no space for other creative thoughts. You end up in losing precious time, which can never be earned again.

Swami Vivekanand says, "The whole secret of existence is to have no fear. Never fear what will become of you, depend on no one. Only the moment you reject all help, you are freed."

List down all probabilities for failures. Do not hesitate to write the smallest one. Believe in Murphy's law, "Whatever can go wrong, will surely go wrong." Stretch your imagination. Be Devil's advocate. Think all worst possibilities. For time being, let your mind be totally negative. Be complete sadist and pessimistic.

Listed all? Now, coolly read all problems. To your surprise, you will find more than 90% are very easily solvable, 9% do not exist at all and only 1% needs a solution. Brainstorming could resolve this 1% with small efforts. Offer these 1% issues to your team. Have a brainstorming session. You will find an incredible solution.

Henry Ford was passing thru a bad phase. There was fear to be extinct if the engine is not powerful enough. Other competitors were catching up the market share. He used a fantastic technique to resolve his problem. He wanted to increase the power of the car engine. The problem was, the size of the engine was coming out to be really big, resulting in odd shape of the car. Also, from maintenance point of view, the new engine was too problematic. Henry called all his engineers on the project and closed them in a room. The target was to come out of the room only with the correct solution.

The team took few days. But they came out of the room with a design of "V Engine", the most popular arrangement of cylinders till date. This is one of the great innovations of the century.

Troubles are never as serious as they appear. Many times it is your mind that works negatively and develops lot of negative thoughts. The best and simplest ways to face the fear is to face it immediately and upfront. This saves lot of time. There are three probabilities as follows:

1) The fear we think is only the mind game we are playing with ourselves. It is not in existence at all.

2) It exists, but not with the gravity we feel about. Get an idea of degree of seriousness and take necessary steps.

3) If it is in existence and is severe, it is better to start working on the same at earliest. In any case, if it exists, we need to face it one time or the other. Better do it earlier.

In a famous quote, Henry Ford says "If you think you can, or if you think you cannot, either way you are right."

Keep faith in yourself. Entrepreneurship is all about taking risks. Rewards are directly proportional to risk. Also, it is not necessary that you should always win. Failure is a part of life. Do not avoid it. It needs courage to accept the failure. Even if you lose, you earn the experience of why you have not won. This experience will be useful at some other point in life.

Major fear reduces as soon you confront the crisis. So do it at earliest, may be today, just now.

DEMOCRATIC MINDSET

I love democracy, as long as I can afford it...

A first generation entrepreneur, being emotionally attached and possessing fear for existence, always tends to be democratic. He tries to take opinions of every team member and wants to work with consensus. This is of course a very good virtue, as long as it works positively. But at times, if the collective opinion differs from his vision, there is danger of him getting dragged along with the team in a different direction.

To avoid this, the leader should learn to put his foot down at appropriate time. Over democracy is not good for business. Of course, this is not against collective decision making; it is just against getting away from vision and mission of the organisation and the leader.

In all leading democracies of the world, there is only one leader, may be President or Prime Minister or Chancellor or Fuhrer or whatever you call. Any organisation, may be a country or company, runs efficiently, if there is a single leader. Many cooks will always spoil the cook.

We see organisations collapsing if multiple leaderships emerge. Any two individuals will have difference of opinion. Two power centres are detrimental.

Following the instructions without questioning, is a sign of good follower. Working together wholeheartedly irrespective of difference of opinions is a characteristic of a winning team.

Democratic mindset, sometimes, is outcome of introvert nature of the leader. His shyness and accommodative nature does not permit him to tell the team members courageously about their mistakes. This is harmful for the organisation.

Remember your school days. There is a "Class Representative" in the class. Normally, he / she are the person who may not be the best in academics, but has a power to administrate. One who can dictate and keep the whole class silent. In simple words, he can control the class and report to his higher authority, the teacher. This is a basic example of organisational democracy. One amongst the group becomes the leader and controls the organisation.

Even in our day to day life, we find that the assertive persons are more visible and more popular. They have the guts to speak the truth, however bitter it is. Also, they can face the opposition of the colleagues / superiors to prove their point. As long as this happens in the interest of the organisation, they surely succeed in long run.

Every organisation needs a leader. It is first responsibility of the leader to build a team which has a faith in him. If team does not have faith in him, over democracy will follow. Take example of any successful organisation. It succeeded only because of the strong leader. The strong leader is one who has a vision, who believes in himself and his team and above all, has guts to swim against the stream.

Once the team is built, it is simple to achieve goals. A little autocracy always adds a great value. Autocratic leaders also make mistake, give wrong instructions and make incorrect decisions. Do not worry. Good team has a capability to overcome all eventualities.

Two of the most successful organisations till date are General Electric and Apple. GE was in deep crisis and it is turned around by Jack Welch. The critics comment that some of the methods used by Jack are reckless and inhuman. He is blamed for his autocracy. Even if we accept this in toto, fact remains! Jack had given results. If he would not have done what he did, today probably GE would have been a history. Not to forget, GE has multiple million of families dependent on it and above all, it has a large contribution in the economy of The US. Rather than saying Jack ruthlessly removed some people, we should say he saved many people, GE and USA.

Finally results will speak. In any organisation, democracy beyond a point is detrimental. This is not an endorsement of autocratic management. This simply means that if required, one has to be strong enough to take decisions against the majority and carry it successfully.

ALIGNMENT OF WORKFORCE

None of us is as smart as all of us.
Ken Blanchard

Inside the organisation, each one should be aware of the goals of the company. These goals are all type of goals. They are sales targets, new product launching dates, old product phase out plans, inventory reduction targets, profitability ratios etc etc....

Short, medium and long term business plans should be shared with all stakeholders. Awareness of future plans and past performances is a requisite. This helps in bringing alignment.

Business is nothing less than a tug war. Other end is pulled by numerous difficulties. Our end is stronger if and only if our internal strengths are good and all are aligned to pull in same direction.

During starting phase, non-alignment results in excessive and undue efforts to achieve goals. A famous quote says, "If you want to be incrementally better, be competitive. If you want to be exponentially better, be cooperative."

Alignment brings great results. Jack Welch names his book, "Who says elephants can't dance?" With proper alignment of workforce, elephants can dance. GE is one of the best examples of success through alignment of workforce.

One of the best examples of success thru team efforts is Japan after World War II. The country was completely ruined. Atomic energy proved its power of destruction. Unfortunately Japan was the victim. It is the country where every essential commodity is to be imported. No land, no natural resources, no food grains, not even enough drinking water. Apart from forced calamities, it is the most earthquake prone region. Whole country aligned on development. In a short span of 30 years, they emerged as one of the noticeable economy in the world.

As an organisation, we were passing thru a bad phase. In spite of having good customer base, state of the art infrastructure, wide management bandwidth, we unable to attract desired speed of growth. Neither top line was growing nor was bottom line looking attractive. We studied the phenomenon of other big industrial houses. The observation was the bottom most person in the successful organisation was talking the same language as the top management. We were surprised to notice a peculiar point in a company with highest Earning before interest, tax, depreciation and apportioning (EBITDA) in terms of percentage, in its sector, on global level. The methodology adopted to align the people is very interesting:

1) Decide areas of focus. E.g. Quality, Cost, Productivity, Business Development etc.
2) Set targets for each area E.g.

Sr No.	Area	Target (e.g.)
a)	Quality	<100 ppm
b)	Cost	<12%
c)	Productivity	>97%
d)	Business Development	>35%
e)	Manpower reduction	>20%
f)	EBITDA	>15%
g)	Abc………..	
h)	Xyz………..	

Explain these Key Result Areas to each and every employee, from top to bottom.

3) Distribute above KRAs in small tasks and enlist all of them.
4) As per the importance of each area, formulate a marking system.
5) Evaluate the performance of each individual based on this system.
6) This evaluation is to be related with annual assessment and in turn with annual increment.
7) The system will be more effective if you can introduce a "Variable Pay" system. A portion in the payment is variable. This variable pay is to be given after monthly / quarterly / half yearly assessment, based on performance.

This is the blend of performance v/s reward. If this system can be made more objective, it will have an excellent result. Motivation for performance and fear of losing money goes hand in hand and supplements each other positively. This helps in making over all alignment of each individual with organisational goals.

Once people are aligned, everything starts moving in right direction. Collective wisdom prevails. Otherwise difficult targets are now simpler and impossible tasks are now visible.

COMMUNICATION

The greatest problem in communication is the
illusion that it has been accomplished.
George Bernard Shaw

Communication is a subject of its kind. You will find numerous literatures on the subject. Many authorities commented on the topic in great details. Here we will discuss only about an organisation, which is in "Start" phase, i.e. an organisation in nascent stage.

As all of us are aware, in any organisation, formal communication is in two forms,

1) Verbal
2) Written

Verbal communication has some limitations.

a) The meaning may not be conveyed effectively. If the "Convener" and the "Listener", both or either are not in the respective mode, the perception differs, resulting in distorted communication.

b) There is no record. This gives flexibility to both stakeholders, leading to different versions of same communication.

c) Rate of distortion of communication is very high at each step of verbal communication. More are the steps, more is the distortion. If the steps are more than five, the whole communication is distorted upside down.

Written communication has different issues than verbal communication.

  a) Interpretational problems are more in written communication. Each one tries to interpret whatever is most convenient to him.

  b) The same can be used as a record, for the issue which is out of context.

Communication in the organisation is not only by words, emails or text exchanges. According to all time great Management Guru, Peter Drucker, "The most important thing in communication is hearing what isn't said". It is reading between lines. It can be non verbal. It can be thru acts and deeds. Body language is used to communicate. Moreover, many times, no communication is also a communication. Pitch of your say and tone of your voice changes the meaning upside down. Facial expressions, body postures and eye movements speak your mind. Your tongue can speak different things than what your eyes say.

Some characteristics of written communication converse a lot. Written statements are treated as commitments. Your writing reflects your personality. It is an indication of your status, your intelligence and your knowledge. Grammatical mistakes are sign of your poor acumen. Incorrect exhortation creates a bad impression. If you are communicating by email, be cautious about organizational hierarchy of the other side. Addressing a senior with a copy marked to junior is discourteous. It should be other way round. While writing to anybody, categorically avoid harsh language. Nothing is so simple that it cannot be misunderstood.

Harsh words are misunderstood very easily and much loudly. Always be well-mannered on paper.

Good internal communication results in smooth and harmonious work. Communication is depositing a part of you in another person. Once this deposition takes place in every person, synergy is induced. This synergy drives the organisation in right direction to achieve desired milestones. Enlisted are some indicators of an organisation with a good internal communication:

1) Everyone greets the other person with a smile irrespective of hierarchical position. While passing by, they exchange few words with each other.
2) Absence on work or casual leaves is prior sanctioned. People adjust amongst themselves in case of date clashes.
3) Sick leaves are well intimated.
4) Any subordinate can meet any boss without appointment.
5) There are frequent informal gatherings.
6) The children of the colleagues are friends of each other. There is a family bond.
7) Car sharing is common.
8) "In" punching of cards is dot before time.

If internal communication is not good, everyone follows his own policy. Company vision is not adhered to. The goals are not achieved. Financial statements start deteriorating. Customer complains increase. Flow of repeat orders starts dropping. These are the indicators of dire internal communication. Other than this the common indicators are as follows:

1) "Out" punching is dot in time.
2) After office hours, boss is not told formally about going home.
3) Very high level of written communication. This is mainly used as a proof of communication.
4) Frequent use of the phrases "That's not my job." "Too much of politics here".
5) No. of incidences of arguments.

Apart from above five, the reverse of all eight points for good internal communication do exist.

To have good and strong internal communication, the real solution is to inculcate well built management systems with clearly defined roles and goals. The major reason for bad communication are grey areas in responsibility and authority. If these grey spots are eliminated, half of the work is done. The written down muscular management systems will take care of remaining half, thanks to well articulated Japanese management system like Toyota Production System or globally accepted ISO system. These are formulated after in depth study of various global scenarios of excellent management. One can adopt any such system as per his convenience.

DELEGATION

Believing everybody is dangerous;
believing nobody is very dangerous...
Abraham Lincoln

One person might be skilful enough to perform a job of two. But with proper delegation, he can surely make thousands of persons to perform. Do you agree? This is the power of delegation.

If you started the business and are striving for success, delegation is one of the important aspects. No single thing is worse than non-delegation. Normally, first generation entrepreneurs avoid delegation. There are some dilemmas which make them stay away from delegation. Some of the feelers are:

- ➤ My subordinates are very slow.
- ➤ I want everything perfect.
- ➤ If my subordinate performs better, my importance will descend.
- ➤ My subordinate is a potential threat to my position.
- ➤ My subordinate will develop direct relations with Customers.
- ➤ My subordinate will develop direct relations with the Boss.
- ➤ My subordinate will develop direct relations with Other Stakeholders.

Consider first two causes. Here you have a feeler that you are far better than He / She is. Just imagine, if He / She are fast and perfect, he/she would have already occupied your chair. They are your subordinates because they are slow and imperfect. It is your duty to make them fast, perfect and raise them to your expected level. If they remain slow and imperfect, you will always be overloaded. Neither they nor you will be able to go to the next level.

If you want them to be perfect, let them practice. Practice makes man perfect. Delegation automatically gives them work, in turn practice. Let them make mistakes. Mistakes enrich with experience.

Consider other four causes. Here you have a feeler that they are far better than you. These excuses are worthless for two reasons:

1) No one can be stopped from progressing. If you try to stifle the fire, it will blaze bigger. If the fire is propelled in right direction, it will work miracles for you.

2) A real manager is one who can manage the people smarter than him.

If they are better, they will surely find their way and grow. Better help them growing. Together with themselves, they will make the organisation grow. They might opt for some other job in long run. That won't matter as in long run, on some mode of life, they may help you. Keep them on your networking arena.

Remember, if one has to grow up on the ladder, he has to first create a situation where he himself is completely dispensable. Indispensability is a hurdle for growth. One cannot leave his routine if he is indispensable. Your routine should not consume more than 20% of your time. 80% time should necessarily be spent on planning of future growth. Delegation is the best tool for this.

Delegation brings in expertise and proficiency. However great the Boss is, He / She is never a Superman. He / She could not do everything with high efficacy. Most of the times, subordinates are master in their respective jobs as they do it day in and day out. They can delight with their expertise. Their ideas may prove much better than what we think.

Subordinates are a reflection of the Boss. Good Boss will have better subordinates. Mediocre subordinates represent ordinary average Boss. Subordinates are upgraded only by delegation. Delegation need to be supported by monitoring. A good Boss delegates generously. He stands by the subordinate. He inculcates all required qualities in his subordinates and makes them capable of replacing him. Express your trust on subordinates as United states army general famously said, "Never tell people how to do things. Tell them what to do and they will surprise you with their ingenuity."

PLANNING BEYOND HORIZON

The empires of the future are empires of the mind.
Winston Churchill

During starting phase of business, however small it is, plan for something which is not visible today. It might be completely absurd! Let it be! Does not matter. Miracles do happen. And only common people make them happen.

LN Mittal, from a small family, becomes Steel tycoon producing majority of steel in the world. Losing everywhere throughout life, Abraham Lincoln becomes most popular President of USA. Are these not the miracles? These people always looked beyond horizon. They dreamed, believed and achieved.

Bible says, without a dream, people perish. The greatest danger for most of us is not that our aim is too high and we miss it, but that it is too low and we reach it. Dhirubhai Ambani, when working as a delivery boy on a petrol pump in Eden, SA, did not dream to be an owner of a petrol pump. His dream was to be an owner of an oil company. Steve Jobs dream was to make the life easier for people. See the achievement!

Looking beyond horizon widens your vision. Without vision, your organisation is blind. It runs like a car without headlights, driven in dark night. And trust me, you are not Batman!

LEARN TRICKS OF TRADE

Learn the trade; tricks of the trade will follow.

Every business or profession has its own tricks to play skilfully. We need to learn those in starting phase itself. Delay may be disastrous. These tricks can be learned though three Gurus.

➤ Peers,
➤ Subject Books
➤ Actual Functioning

Unlearning is one of the important parts of learning. Your previous experience may become a stumbling block. Experience of Marketing will not hold water in Operations and engineering experience will fall short in Logistics.

When First Generation Entrepreneur starts a new business or a professional holds new office, he has to unlearn certain stuff, relearn some topics in new context and learn some new modules.

The typical topics to unlearn and relearn with respect to old and new assignments are:

• Work environment
• Relationship with Customer /Boss and Stakeholders
• Customer chemistry
• Product Marketing Strategies
• Organisation Culture

New learning necessarily contains:
- Complete Product Profile
- Market Environment
- Product Cost Structure

Business is not only about selling products. It is a conglomerate of number of business processes. All business processes should be studied. Every business has its own characteristics. Even two plants under same management, manufacturing same product at different locations, demonstrate different trade secrets of success. One has to find out and act upon.

External environment of any business plays a vital role. Learning of external factors affecting business is essential. Customer understanding is one of the important factors. There are examples of business empire debacle if one does not understand the customer. Kodak is one of the best such examples.

Till early 2000's, Kodak was The Name for photography and allied equipments. It was roaring with major share of business, globally. Word photography was becoming synonymous to Kodak. In early 2000, Kodak developed digital photography and digital cameras. However, probably, it could not smell forthcoming change. In spite of developing the technology, it was under the influence of triumph resulting in contentment. This gratification grounded them. Today they are on the verge of economic failure. Hence learning tricks of the trade is a requirement of big companies also, especially during change.

MANAGE YOUR TIME

Until we can manage time,
we can manage nothing else.
Peter F. Drucker

A good Manager is evaluated based on his time management.

Time is the only resource, which everyone possesses equally. Each of us has 24 hours in a day, seven days in a week and 365 days in a year. Then why only few reach high altitudes and rest remain run of the mill? Why only handful businesses grow multinational? Do they have superpowers? Does Almighty bless them more than us? Do they have special brains? The answer is no! Everyone is equal. The difference is how each of us utilises the time.

Time is considered as the fourth dimension. There are lot of scientific theories derived by Albert Einstein and Stephen Hawkins. According to them, there is practically no time lapse if one travels with a speed more than that of light. Apply the same in life. Travel with a speed more than speed of light. There will be no lapse of time!

Time management begins with planning. Plan your day, hour and minute. Identify your time stealers. Normally on the workplace, following are the time stealers:

- Reading emails and replying immediately. This keeps you busy for the whole day and there is lack of concentration. So every work takes more time.

- Over communication on cell phone.
- Writing lengthy emails. Be precise. Master an art of writing short courteous mails. Convey your ideas in minimum words.
- Conducting meetings without agenda. This drags meetings in various directions without giving productive results.
- Frequently calling subordinates in cabin. This may save a little time of yours, but it breaks the link of your subordinate hampering his work quality.
- Reaching late in meetings. This steals time of the others, who are present in time.
- To manage the time more effectively, use following techniques:
- DWM (Daily Works Management). DWM is a very useful and proven practice of managing your time. Numbers of DWM formats are available. However, the best format is to enlist all activities and allocate time to each of them.
- Every meeting should be with a purpose. Circulate the purpose and agenda well in advance. This helps everyone to come prepared.
- Respect time of others. Be disciplined for time. If Boss follows time, others will automatically follow.
- Use electronic gazettes sparingly. Don't be fanatic with it. None of these were available 10 years back. Still you were efficient.

Steve Jobs is the best example who utilised the time most efficiently. He lived for 55 years. First 20 years were in childhood and adolescence, where he had to fight for survival, as he was almost an orphan. Last 10 years he was fighting against medical problems. In the middle 25 years, he was thrown out from the company where he was a founder. He was away for @ 15 years from the company. Effectively, he got only 10 quality years to work. All his creation is in these 10 years. Amazing! Isn't it? This is the difference effective time utilisation makes!

START

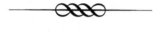

External

MARKET

Good companies will meet needs. Great companies will create market.
Philip Kotler

In the starting of business, market plays a vital role in external environment. A beginner will always think, "I can make this, but who will buy it?" Where is the market?

Honourable Ms. Golda Meir, 4th Prime Minister of Israel and World's 3rd Woman Prime Minister, popularly known as Iron Lady of Israel, quotes, "The dog that trots around finds a bone."

If you are in beginning phase and trying to find the market, following tips could be useful:

- Identify your core competence. It will give you the track of available market. It is always simpler to start with own core competence. You can play on this. You know what to do and how to do. The probability of success increases tenfold.
- Identify hobby which gives you pleasure. Think on business opportunities related to the same. Business emerging out of hobby is always very successful and delighting. By default, you try to do your best. Work becomes fun. Every moment is joyous. Working time is no constraint. That's precisely the reason why Michel Jackson was

successful in singing dancing and Sachin Tendulkar is World's greatest cricketer.

- Identify the waves in market environment. Study the related business trend. Enlist opportunities. Identify what you can do.
- Try, try and try.

Winston Churchill famously said, "Success is not final, failure is not fatal: it is the courage to continue that counts."

Scientific studies prove that 5% success rate is considered as a high success rate. Whether this 5% is first or last, depends on your effort level and destiny.

Law of conservation of energy states "Energy cannot be created nor it can be destroyed." Law of conservation of market is exactly opposite. "Market can be created and destroyed depending on the passion you put into."

Market is either identified or created. Identification of market is simpler as it already exists and one has to just tap it. Naturally the law of low risk low reward applies. Existing market will always be competitive, resulting in less return. Whereas, created market will account for more risk, hence more reward.

DO'S AND DO NOT'S

Direction is more important than speed

Once you start the business, two probabilities exist:
- There are abundant opportunities
- There is a scarcity of opportunities.

When you have plenty of opportunities, there is a danger of losing the core values resulting in a loss of direction. This is the time to be cautious. To succeed at earliest, one would always like to en-cash every opportunity. There can be short term gains, but long term losses may prevail.

In start phase, direction is very important. As this is the beginning, speed may not matter much. You can cover the gap later. But missing the direction may impact in long run. You will reach a destination, which you never intended. Then you will lose interest. Loss of interest will affect your performance in growth phase. One cannot work effectively if he is not involved in it mentally. Involvement is a product of interest.

We can see a number of people around us, who are capable but do not perform. The only reason is they are not involved in their work. It is interesting to understand if they have lost the direction in start phase of the activity.

If there is scarcity of opportunity on what you have decided, be sure that you are on right path. Go on searching. Do not lose your heart. Grabble the untrodden path. You will find one. Probably, this path might be new and virgin. As you take longer to find it, others also will take more time. So there will be lesser competition. You will get advantage of being the first guy in the queue. Hence, Probability of success will increase.

An idea of making hamburgers available in numbers of places might be a stupid idea in 1940's. Today we call it McDonalds. Making a wonderland and cartoon films was supposedly a foolish concept in 1923. Now people call it Disney Land. Pulling a cart without horse was unbelievable. Presently cars are a mandatory part of our life.

If there is a scarcity of opportunities, related to your concept, it only means there is opportunity to do something different. In his famous quote, a motivational speaker Shiv Khera says, "Winners don't do different things, they do the things differently."

There is no need to reinvent the wheel. Just find yours and apply it to your lorry. Don't waste your precious time. Presently all technologies are available. Just find the appropriate one and apply it to your concept.

A Not To Do list is as important as a To Do list. Prepare the list. Stick it on your pin up board. Read it every day. Memorize it by heart. This is also a guide line for future.

We come across a lot of people who say. "Bro, this is not what I wanted to do in my life. My dream was to be a …………..". Certainly they had forgotten to tag the Not To Do list on their pin up boards. In the start phase, such people lose their direction, ending up in doing what they do not want to do. You will be one of them. Be vigilant. A so called opportunity may be a trap of destiny to test your willpower. Do not be a victim of the fate.

FIERCE COMPETITION

Fittest will survive
Charles Darwin

Competition is for survival. Fittest will survive. How can you or me change the law of nature? Wherever there is a business, competition is unavoidable. Honey attracts ants. You are not the only person on this earth who senses the opportunity. There are others too, may be better than you. Everyone wants to win. All are capable. Competition is inevitable.

Competition is good. It keeps you alert. It makes you work. It does not permit you slumber. It makes you think. It is instrumental to distinguish you from others.

Unhealthy competition is better. I do not advice to start unhealthy competition from your side. But if you encounter with the competitor coming with unhealthy competition, trust me it will prove good for your betterment. You learn the hard realities faster. You become tougher. So be happy if someone makes unhealthy competition with you. He is teaching you lessons of life. You will emerge as a more powerful and wise individual. One cycle of unhealthy competition will train you to face bigger challenges. You will be stronger than ever before.

Jealousy is love! It is love in competition. It will happen. There is no exception.

Exactly reverse will happen if you play unfair game with your competitor. He will be in commanding mode. Do not take that risk.

In a very interesting quote Jarod Kintz says "Competition is healthy. Especially when all your competitors are unhealthy, and hopefully sick and absent during the competition."

Everyone knows his business. Each one has the capability to survive and grow. Nobody can stop others from moving forward.

Above all, if some casualty is to happen due to unhealthy competition, it will happen anyways. If you are not the fittest, you will vanish and unhealthy competition will be just one of the excuses. There will be a number of such excuses, even otherwise. So, be amongst the fittest club of Darwin.

Competition in business or profession is not like Olympics or Asian Games. There competition ends as the games are over. Here it is unending. To win this chase, difference of 0.1 seconds in first and second is not enough. You have to be miles ahead of the competitor. Otherwise you don't know when others will outshine you. Attitude must be to win and not "not to lose".

CUSTOMER RELATIONS MANAGEMENT

Unless you are miles ahead of competition, meet people and stroke a few egos regularly

What is a customer? Is it an organisation? A company? A department? No way! Customer is the person dealing with you. An individual. A human being. He / She has emotions and feelings. He / She gets angry. He / She can be pleased. He / She has personal issues and problems in office.

Managing Customer Relations is simple. Identify the needs. If categorised, the needs are as follows:

- Cost : This is a one time need. It appears to be much more important than actual. We thrust very high on this, whereas from customer perspective, value of the product is more important than cost.

- Value : Value defines the cost. Higher the value, higher is the cost and more are the margins. Add value to your product, cost will follow.

- Delivery : Timely delivery is what all customers want mandatorily. If delivery is delayed, customer may buy if he has some compulsions, but will surely lose his faith and start looking for other supplier.

- Quality : In changing scenario of globalisation, best quality products are available on every nook and corner. Customer is aware of quality. Gone are the days to differentiate export quality from indigenous quality. Bad quality products will be replaced in no time.

These are tangible or direct needs. There are some intangible needs also.

- Ego : Never touch the ego of your customer. If ego is hurt, the customer is lost forever. Whatever you do, customer will not turn back.
- Body language: Customer is the boss. First rule - Boss is always right. Second rule - If Boss is wrong, follow rule no. 1. Behave courteously with the customer. Monitor your body language. Watch your words. Mind your tone. Control your postures!
- Personal Space: Whatever closeness you share with your customer, give him a personal space. Do not try to enter in his kitchen. Little distance maintains balance of respect for each other. Intimacy increases expectations, which could be far away from reality.
- Communication: Frequent communication will refresh the relations while communication gap will increase the coldness. Out of sight is out of mind. Be visible! Visibility is not necessarily seen only by eyes. It is seen thru fulfilment of tangible needs and felt via discharging intangible requirements. It is seen on emails, courtesy calls and casual greets.

- Customer Delight: Try to add value in the services or products which will delight the customer. That will set you apart from others. Be a brand! A preferred one!

FORECAST THE WEATHER

Climate is what we expect, weather is what we get.
Mark Twain

Keep your antennas open. Exert your senses. Correct prediction of external weather will tell you which crops will yield better.

The only permanent thing is change. Change needs agents. In business, sensitivity quotient is very high. Any small variation will change the weather. Skill lies in forecasting the same before time.

There are examples of organisations which do not sense changing climate and enter into doldrums. Even a small delay leads to incur huge losses.

Take any company, lasting for more than half century; the major reason for its longevity is ability to respond quickly to external environment.

The major reasons for not responding can be categorised as follows:
- Complacency
- Resistance to change
- Not stepping out of comfort zone
- Fear of losing
- Dislike towards the job
- Too much engrossment in routine work
- Losing the focus

Reasons for change in environment can be:

- Change of person at the customer's end
- Change of organisation structure at the customer's end
- Change of person at our end
- Change of organisation structure at our end
- Taste of customer
- Internal processes
- Government policies
- Economic conditions of the country
- Economic conditions on Global level

GROWTH

Personal

TECHNICAL V/S COMMERCIAL

Good CEOs are not necessarily good businessmen.

It is frequently heard that "He is a core technical guy," especially about some first generation entrepreneurs. Watch those businesses. Are they financially undisciplined? Are their bankers cautious while offering facilities to them? Are they not growing up to their fullest potential? In majority of the cases, answer is yes!

Core competence can be technical. It is very good for starting phase of business to understand what to do and how. Simultaneously, during growth, understanding commercials is must. Business is not all, but a lot about money. Understanding health of business is essential. Healthy business needs financial discipline. One needs to know the financial ratios and understand bottom lines. Reserves and surplus define the life cycle of an organisation.

In your business plan, apart from production and sales targets, set goals for EBITDA and PBT. Plan short term, medium term and long term objectives for current ratio, quick ratio and debt equity ratio.

Review your financial statements frequently. Respect your Chartered Accountant as you respect your family doctor. Have monthly check ups with him. Undergo stress tests with regular frequency.

Keep a watch on the factors affecting health of your organisation.

Many organisations face issues during growth. A very common problem is using short term loans for long term application. This disturbs the financials completely. There are number of such issues which affect the health of business adversely. Take care of them. If commerce is your weakness, start working on it. This is also your job. Be a master in commerce may it be with or without a formal degree…

Normally, for any business, commerce is a subject of only five algebraic operations, addition, subtraction, multiplication division and percentage. You know all about this. It is simple for you. Your consultant will take care of rest complicated matters.

Just to cross check my observations, read the annual reports of companies listed on share market. See the Annexure of List of Directors / major shareholders. Look for their educational qualifications. In majority of the cases, there is a definite mismatch in qualifications and actual portfolios. You may find a Commercial Graduate as the Technical Director, Chartered Accountant as Managing Director, Arts graduate taking care of Finance and so on. This indicates that an entrepreneur has to be versatile. Being only technical or only commercial may not help.

You need not be the master of all. Hire the people smarter than you. This is elaborated in a previous chapter. Important thing is technical as well as commercial competence of your organisation. The leader has to understand at least basics of both the things. Being only "Technical" or only "Commercial" is not good for the health of the organisation.

COMPLACENCY

When a great team loses through complacency,
it will constantly search for new and more
intricate explanations to explain away defeat
-Pat Riley Quotes

A very common hurdle in growth is complacency. Pride of achievement is biggest enemy of growth! This pride brings in complacency. Complacency leads to stagnancy. Stagnancy is beginning of de-growth. De-growth pilots perishing of organisation.

Pride of achievement
⇩
Complacency
⇩
Stagnancy
⇩
De-growth
⇩
Organisation perishes

If you want to grow, first decide your targets. Let the targets be stretched, very stretched. They should seem to be almost impossible. Follow Walt Disney: "It's a kind of fun to do impossible." Start chasing them. They will come closer. You will start visualising the same. As soon as visibility is closer, revise your targets. Again repeat the process. Be on the toes. Always!

Apparently, this seems theoretical and impractical. Believe me, it is not. Once you start practising this, you will start enjoying this. It is like playing a game. Continuous monitoring automatically brings passion. Small achievement gives great pleasure. Pleasure brings motivation. Motivation boosts enthusiasm. Enthusiasm again increases passion. It is a circle, not vicious but vivacious!

The major reason for debacle of most of the first generation businesses is complacency. First generation entrepreneur tends to be complacent in growth stage. In start phase, he has nothing to lose. May be he is at such a stage where he will win or be where he is! Hence risk taking is relatively easy.

During growth stage, he has already achieved something! So now there is a fear to lose. This fear acts as a dragging force to move forward.

Here, count your successes. Look back at your start phase. As you have guts, you could start being an entrepreneur. You took risks and enjoyed rewards. Now to go to higher level, you have to take higher risks. There are no free lunches. Today's success is tomorrow's routine. Tomorrow another success is necessary. Remember, doing business is like riding a bicycle. It will either move forward or will fall down. Carrying it and walking side by is more painful. Always ride it, pedal and move forward. Never be complacent. Be happy with your achievements, but never be satisfied with them!

HEALTH MANAGEMENT

To keep the body in good health is a duty... otherwise we shall not be able to keep our mind strong and clear.
Buddha

Being an entrepreneur is not a cakewalk. There are lot of frills attached. One has to enter into number of unknown areas. Risk taking becomes part of life. This invites a lot of mental and physical stresses. To withstand these, one has to maintain the health. Sound mind resides only in sound body.

Watch the physique of great people in news or great people in history. A very common factor is good health. The great performers are always fit and fine. If you don't believe me, just watch the body tone of Barack Obama, Amitabh Bachchan, Sachin Tendulkar, Kiran Bedi, Abraham Lincoln, Sonu Nigam, Shakira, Ratan Tata, Bill Gates or anyone else who you think are successful in life...

Commonly seen problem in growth phase is absolutely incorrect lifestyle. Late wake up, no work out, irregular diet, late night parties and so on. Growth phase is the most stressful period in whole lifecycle of any business (and this phase should be perpetual).

In this period, Health Management is sidelined with a very common excuse, "No time". One, who does not spare quality time for himself, can never upgrade himself. Time spent in health management is an investment, giving very high returns. It pays back very rich dividends. Be religious to spend time on work outs. Do it regularly. Have regular health checkups.

Your body always talks to you. Listen to it carefully. It gives clear indications of what it wants. Respond positively. Do not stretch it beyond limits. Overloading physically reflects into poor mental response. Incorrect decision making will take away much more than what you earn by excessive stretching. Business or profession is a mind game. Stressed body means stressed mind. To keep your mind open, your body should be stress free.

Human body has tremendous capacity. It adjusts itself above 55 ^{0}C in Sahara desert and -25 ^{0}C in Antarctica. It survives in zero gravity space for months together and can walk on Moon where gravity is 1/6th of Earth. This is possible for all of us if we are physically fit. Our routine requirements of working are much easier when compared to above tasks. If we keep ourselves fit, we can take much more load on ourselves what we are taking today. The efficiency will reach its highest level. The quality of decision will be better, hence results will be better. The performance will reach to peak.

Bear in mind, Health Management is KRA no. 1 (Key result area no.1), always. If your score is 100% for this KRA, you need not worry on other KRAs. They will automatically improve.

MERCY KILLS

Surprised with the title? Even after enormous head scratching, I could not find a suitable quote beneath the title. Unfortunately the title is true in business or profession. Any merciful decision may prove detrimental in business. As I said earlier, business or profession is not all, but a lot about money. Mercy involves emotions. Emotions do not care for money and not caring for money is not business. In nutshell, mercy kills business.

Common merciful act is absorbing nears and dears as employees, especially in key positions. As long as this decision is based on merit, it is fine. But if this is an emotional decision, you are a pray! The issue worsens when the performance is not up to the mark and you cannot reflect due to long or personal relationship. During growth phase, speed is important and the same is hampered in this case. The organisation starts bleeding. Overall performance deteriorates and customers vanish.

Business is not grown by people; it is grown by right people.

A typical phenomenon of "Corporate Social Responsibility" during growth phase is very interesting.

When an entrepreneur or professional is passing through growth time, he has already tested success. He is roaming in dreamland and sometimes walking few inches above the ground. Initial success gives a feeler of conquering the world. He starts feeling society as his responsibility and wants to lead in cleaning up the society. His social activities increase. There is a danger of losing focus in this compassion. Focussing more on peripheral activities mercifully may lead to long term irreparable damages to core activity.

Important point to be noted here: Nothing wrong in taking social responsibilities, but only after sustenance phase of business. Growth period demands your absolute attention.

LOOK YOURSELF IN GROWN SHOES

"I am the greatest. And I said it before I knew it."
Mohammed Ali

A first generation entrepreneur, on growing path, always has a dilemma, "Can I do this?" He is entangled in his past. He compares the past with present and blushes on his success. This blushing impedes the passion. He enters in protection mode, protecting what is achieved! Future plans are side tracked. Outcome is mediocrity.

Start looking yourself in bigger shoes, shoe you want to wear after three – five - ten years. Act today as if you have reached medium term or long term goals. Believe in yourself. Tell yourself that you can do it! If you want to be a multimillionaire, behave like one. Do not worry what others say. Abraham Lincoln said "Your own resolution to succeed is most important than any other thing.

Mind is a very powerful gift of nature. As Henry Ford said, if you think you can and if you think you cannot, you are right. All time great boxer Mohammed Ali said "I am the greatest, and I said it much before I knew it." That is the confidence. Dreams with eyes open will always come true.

Here is an anecdote of a legendary man, the second Minister of Finance of independent India, Mr. C.D.

Deshmukh. In his early days, after completion of University education, he appeared for Civil Services Exams. The day results declared, his friend rushed to find him. After spotting him on a regular badminton court, with sheer excitement, he told Mr. Deshmukh that results were out. The cool question from other side was "Oh! Who ranked second?"

See the amazing confidence!

In Indian mythology, Dhruva was a son of a King. The King had two Queens. The step mother of young Dhruva insulted him and pulled out from cuddle of the King. Dhruva pledged to achieve an irrevocable place with his holy deeds. His devotion and untiring efforts won boon of God to become a Pole Star. As we know, Pole Star never changes the location. It is immovable.

Be a Pole Star!!!

Train your mind to look yourself from outside. Tell your mind that you can do whatever you think. Poets and writers often dreamed to reach the moon. Just a fictional thought in late 60's. But it happened! Subsequently Mars is triumphed. Now Lunarregistry. com is selling plots on moon and people are buying. Amazing! They are looking themselves as residents of The Moon. Soon, Neil Armstrong and Michael Jackson won't be amongst the rare persons to do the Moonwalk...

One of the great ancient Emperors in India, Chandragupta, was from a poor farmer's family. During his childhood, playing with his buddies, he never accepted any role less than a king. He was always wearing the grown shoes. Finally the dream came true.

Dreaming does not cost. Not dreaming does! This cost is invisible but takes away lot of precious and golden time in life. Like a pro-businessman, make sure to negotiate with this cost as much as you can...

LEARN MANAGING FUNDS

Money is like sixth sense and you can't
use the other five without it
William Somerset Maugham

The first sign of success for a First Generation Entrepreneur is his fat bank balance. And here starts a race of exploring new avenues of income.

The first slip is about bank balance. One has to understand the bank balance is not the indicator of ownership of this money. The money in your account has many owners. You are only the custodian of this money.

The first and foremost owner is Government. Any organisation has to discharge the liabilities as per law of the land. Many times, it needs self declaration. There is a tendency to take undue advantage of this. This cash is utilised for other use, much less important the real priorities.

The second important owners are your own employees. They are with the organisation as organisation takes care of them. The day organisation stops caring, they will not be with the company, first mentally and then as a formality, physically.

The third essential owners are your bankers. In most of the cases, your financial stake in business is much smaller than your bankers. Financial institutions are the owners of your company in real sense.

Next key owners of the funds in your account are your business partners or suppliers. Major portion of our revenue belongs to the goods supplied by them.

Normal blunder we tend to do is to utilise short term funds for long term investments or using working capital to procure fixed assets. This affects the funds management adversely and one loses on opportunities of new business for unavailability of working capital. In such times, financial institutions also do not help as your financial ratios are unsound.

Earning money is relatively easy. Borrowing money is still easier. On the other hand, right utilisation of money is damn difficult. Value of money lessens when one possesses it. The value is realised when you do not have it. Be careful. You are handling somebody else's money. All of them are watching you. If you do not perform, all above mentioned stakeholders will pull the carpet.

Every dollar, own or borrowed, has a cost attached to it. We call it interest. Count this even if it is your own money. Every day, for a given project, your liabilities should reduce.

Money has a special characteristic of evaporation. If it is not handled properly, it evaporates. It disappears in air. It vanishes in any direction. Analysis and fault finding is just equivalent to post-mortem after death.

We come across number of families and individuals telling stories of their rich ancestral heritage. Are they the victims of improper management of funds by their peers?

LEAD FROM FRONT

*A leader is one who knows the way, goes
the way, and shows the way*
John Maxwell

No war can be won if the Chief is absent from war field. History witnessed this numerous times. Morale of the soldiers is high when the leader is demonstrating his leadership, visibly or invisibly. His presence must be felt. The presence can be physical or in terms of moral support or in the form of motivation.

Napoleon Bonaparte is registered in history as he was an idol for his disciples. He was staying amongst them, eating amongst them and was always ahead on battlefield. Similar is the case of Alexander the Great.

In organisation, everyone watches you. You being in the senior position, your every act is analysed. People from their opinion based on what they see about you and not by what you talk about yourself.

Flattering teammates may not necessarily create a good impression and bullying in limits does not necessarily create a bitter feeling. If the Boss is logical and unbiased, people are ready to breathe their last for him. We see number of examples of turnaround of chapter 11 or bankrupt companies. The essential reason for such success is the ability of the leader to lead from front. General Electric is turned around by Jack Welch and Narayanmurthy started his second innings in Infosys for the same.

If you see the companies growing with leaps and bounce, take it for granted that the leader is leading from front. If the growth rate is average, there is problem in leadership.

Leading from front automatically reflects the aggression of the entrepreneur. This aggression boosts energy in the organisation. The goals are set, achieved and new goals are set. People start running. They start looking beyond horizons. They feel confident about their future. Everyone wants growth. If leader is energetic, he brings synergy in the organisation.

Of course, in management, leading from front does not mean micro management. It is not looking into each small task and giving physical consent to every action. It is not supervising all activities. It simply means creating task friendly atmosphere. It is a regular review. It is guiding at proper stage. It is standing by the people when they make unintended blunders.

AVOID COMPARISON

You shouldn't compare yourself to others. They are more screwed up than you think you are

Comparison is a human tendency. We all are grown comparing ourselves with someone. Right from school days, marking system measures us in on some figures. Our standing is decided on marks or grades in comparison with others. Is comparison, really a correct method to opine about someone?

During growth, one develops a tendency to peep in others deeds. Based on actions of other people, our strategies are formed. This has a major disadvantage. While playing cricket, you should not watch adjacent pitch. Concentrate on your pitch; use your bat to hit the Yorker bowled for you. Otherwise, you will lose your wicket.

Nature is the biggest power on the earth. This nature also cannot manufacture two human beings which are exactly alike. No two individuals can be equal, under any circumstances. Not even twins coming from same mother's womb, at almost same time, are similar. Then what is a fun in comparing with somebody else? There is bound to be a difference.

Twins, born and brought up under same circumstances, nourished by same parents, getting equal opportunities in life, having same backing, having equal monetary support, respond differently for the same situation. Their performances will differ even when they have same circumstances. If this is the scenario, then what is the use of comparing with others?

By comparison, we are offending ourselves. It is underestimating our capabilities. We set very low goals if we compare with someone. We set mediocre benchmark. Instead, decide your own goals! Set your benchmarks! Stretch your imagination! Cross your limits! Do your best! Reset the targets and repeat above steps.

Comparison leads to unrest. It produces stomach-ache piloting ulcers. There are heartaches and heartburns. This affects your mental piece. The outcome is negative thinking. This negation impacts adversely on decision making. Taking wrong decision leads to deterioration of the organisation.

EARLY SUCCESS IS ENEMY

Success is a lousy teacher. It seduces smart people into thinking they can't lose.
Bill Gates

Surprised with the title? It is a tragic truth. Success is not always good. Especially early success may prove detrimental. In Bill Gate's words, it seduces smart people thinking that they cannot lose. This seduction is intoxicating. One goes under the influence of success, especially in early times.

Just watch around. Recollect your memories. Remember your classmates. Surely you know who was always or many times topper in the class. Find out where he is today? Barring few respectable exceptions, are they far away from success compared to the then mediocre classmates?

In most of the cases the reply is positive. It is equally true with your work colleagues who were blue eyed boys in the beginning of career.

This does not mean you should not succeed in earlier phase of life. Life is very short. You should succeed as early as possible. The only care you should take is to handle the success tactfully. One success should not become a foundation for next failure. In success or failure, mindset matters a lot. Seduction that I will never lose, paves a road to fail and fear of losing surely makes you fail.

Handle the success as you handle your enemy. Analyse the success. Find out the main reasons for success. Repeat them to gain the next one. Identify probabilities of failure. Note down what can go wrong. Act upon it. Use SWOT (Strength Weakness Opportunity Threat) analysis.

If you look in the history, there are number of great people who had tremendous potential but could not succeed because they were unable to handle early success. Do not enrol your name in that list. Handle the success delicately. Keep it to your heart. Do not let it penetrate your brain.

FACE THE FEAR
FACTOR FIRST

"Do the thing you fear and the death of fear is certain."
-Ralph Waldo Emerson

Path of growth is full of achievements. Every single business offer, whether small or big, is a new achievement. When you started, you had nothing to lose. So your risk taking ability was high. Now you have something to lose. Will it make you less adventurous?

While walking the way to growth, you often have a lot of first time experiences. You are moving in the unfamiliar area. This is out of your comfort zone. This discomfort brings in fear of the unknown. You are scared to take loan as now you have some assets. You fear to pledge the assets because you are scared of loss in business. You are not adding new customer due to fear of failure on schedules, in turn spoiling hard earned reputation in market.

There is always an existence of fear in competition. There is panic on missed schedules. You are under pressure as a key person left the job amidst of the project. You are nervous as bankers are delaying the loan approval.

You are worried, not only when there is no new project but also if there are ample projects. Anxiety takes hold of you not only if customer does not visit you but also if customer visits you several times.

There are numerous fear factors in business lifecycle. It is a part of life. Do not worry! Face the bigger fear first. Kill it! That will boost your confidence. Then take the next one. Go on till the last fear is killed.

While doing this, you will come across an interesting fact. Problems are not as severe as they appear. On the top, most complex problems have simple solutions.

In Cold War days, The America launched a manned spacecraft. They faced a problem of fountain pen not writing on paper as there is no gravity in space. NASA spent millions of dollars and invented a pen which can write under zero gravity. Great R&D followed by immense success!

Russians were not behind. They launched manned spacecraft much before. They faced same problem. Did they spent huge sum and did R&D? No. They used pencil!!!! Simple solution to complex problem.

Though Michael Faraday identified Benzene in 1825, Its structure was still unknown till 1865 German chemist Friedrich August Kekulé, in his dream, saw serpents holding their tail in mouth, forming a ring. He correlated this for the molecule of Benzene and correctly sorted out a 40 years old complex debate of number of intelligent scientists.

Fear is a state of mind. More you think about it, graver it gets. If you confront, it will run away. Do it earlier.

GROWTH

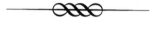

Internal

"ME TOO" CATEGORY

Don't be trapped by dogma, which is living
the result of other people's thinking.
Steve Jobs

Entering in "Me Too" category is one of the dangers during growth phase. This issue is to be considered as an issue related to complete organisation.

Now, you are in phase of growth, where the growth is correlated to top line or total revenue or total sales. Does growth mean only top line or it is also increase in bottom line or profit after tax? Increase in top line makes you bigger but not necessarily stronger. In fact, bottom line is the real measure of strength of your organisation. Growing Big is different from Growing Strong. You have to decide whether you want to grow Big or you want to grow Strong?

During growth phase, keeping top line increase in mind, we tend to grab whatever business comes in. The tendency is to close deals immediately without giving much importance to commercials. This is a trap of entering in "Me Too" category.

Normally, there is abundant business available in bottom of the pyramid. This is lower end of a business, with a huge competition and paper thin margins. Here one has to dance on customer's whims. The business comes in with a great speed and also threat of getting thrown out with double speed. One of the major criterions of business retention is the cost. Lower is the cost; higher is the probability to maintain the business with the company. Even the costs are low, customer demands high quality. As investments are already done, you have no choice. Due to thin margin; the entrepreneur cannot build the organisation or employ smarter people. His maximum time is spent on routine and hardly any time is left for thinking on future establishments. As a result, organisation always struggles to maintain the business with itself. No vision is developed to achieve next level.

Do not let the organisation get entrapped in this situation. Only strong organisations last longer. During growth, keep an eye on bottom line. Growing stronger is much more important than growing bigger. Growing stronger also calls for some cutting edges like technology, special processes, special skills, state-of-the art facilities, project management skills etc. etc.

"Me Too" category gives excellent results temporarily, but in long run, it brands you as a mediocre company. It will not interest new customers. You might be much ahead of the competitors, but you are in a rat race. Even if you win, you will still be a rat!

While growing, organisation should always introspect. New business should be challenged in purview of addition of strengths. Question should be raised whether this business is making us stronger or not.

As a rule of thumb, excellent rate of winning the right business is not more than 10%. Hence in your business plan, plan for ten times of the expected results. This will keep you in a position to choose and not to be chosen. This avoids compulsion.

INDUSTRIAL RELATIONS

Human resources are resources as well as human!

Industrial relations play a vital role in building an organisation. The people will make all the difference! A well built organisation will bring synergy.

Industrial Relation is not synonymous to Industrial Dispute. This term is not meant only for workmen. It is for every human being in the organisation.

One thing everyone needs is appreciation. It is proven by scientific studies that monetary benefits come on second stage for any professional. His first need is recognition and self respect. Everybody wants to grow. Even a sweeper wants appreciation for his job, and if you give it to him, he will try to achieve further excellence in his work. Hence, in industrial relations, appreciation is a key factor.

The second key factor is disciplined and visible leadership. Every subordinate likes a disciplined boss. No one has genuine complains about the strict boss, acting fairly and treating equal to all. Rather, such bosses are highly appreciated. Undisciplined and loose bosses are neither respected nor appreciated. They are always targeted for mockeries in private get togethers. Good industrial relations are maintained better by strict bosses.

A survey by reputed consulting agency shows that 80% industrial relations break due to difference of opinion in boss and subordinate. This indicates that every boss has a pivotal role in IR. The major reason for IR issues is incorrect handling by boss.

Normally the rubbing starts from remuneration. This is the point to be handled very carefully. Important thing is, there has to be an objective assessment system in place. Whatever is to be conveyed to the beneficiary should be conveyed very softly and without hurting him/her. Irrespective of his performance, his self respect should not be ached.

Next point is up-gradation or promotion. Again a transparent assessment system will help. The procedure to be followed is the same.

Salary revisions and up-gradations are normally done once in a year. Give opportunity to the employees to talk. In an open atmosphere, they will share their views and give suggestions, which can be very useful. Listen them carefully. Implement good suggestions. Give credit of such suggestions to individual. This helps in improving ownership of people.

By default, everyone needs appreciation. There are evidences in history that one can lose his life for appreciation from boss. People die to accomplish responsibilities. When it comes on reputation, money, status, position becomes secondary. People love performing. They know, only performance can give recognition. If these feelings are tapped, en-cashed and fed, there is no reason why IR issues would come in picture.

To eliminate IR issues from your company, meet people whenever possible. Do not avoid them. Give them opportunities to perform. Pat their back on every opportunity. Let them feel secured. Encourage them.

Let them participate in various competitions and win the prizes.

In spite of all this, there could be some demands, especially monetary. You have to think coolly on this. Everybody wants more money just like you do! You also always think that the customer is not doing you justice. As being businessmen, we never miss a single chance to demand higher price.

Now, change the shoes and co-relate.

Your subordinate is your supplier and you are his customer. What is wrong if he demands more? What is incorrect if he thinks that you are not doing justice with him? Why should he miss any chance to demand higher price from you? All this is human! It is as same as your thought process. As this thought process is not in your favour, you feel it is incorrect.

This does not mean that every demand will be fulfilled. But keeping cool and thinking from his viewpoint will also give you the correct direction to converse on the demands. After all, you are a big brother and he is your younger family member. Perform that role. To handle human resource, first think of human, resource comes later!

SYSTEM BASED WORKING

Speed is important, Direction is set.

Once you cross the start phase and enters in growth phase, your direction is almost set. Now what is important is speed. This is exactly the reverse of what we discussed in starting phase.

If systems are in place, organisation automatically gains momentum. Accuracy levels in all operations improve, rejections reduce, customer complaints lessen, and ultimately profits increase.

Making systems work in the organisation is a tough job. It needs top down approach. Unless top management is convinced and firm, systems will not fall in place. Hiring a good consultant is not enough. Enforcement of the systems rigorously, is equally important. Getting a certification may be easy, but that will not serve the purpose.

Biggest hurdle to enforce systems is resistance to change. With all odds, people are tuned to some working style. Any change in that style, brings resistance. People have formed their comfort zone. They enjoy predictable problems. They take pride in resolving same problem daily as it makes them specialist of such problems. These problems give them a status of indispensability. Feel of security is hidden behind this indispensability.

Do not compromise on system building. Do it ruthlessly. It should go through in one single attempt.

Do not end first attempt, till goal is accomplished. In every organisation, there are few who have system orientation. Identify and uphold them. Make them responsible. Empower them with authorities. Have regular reviews. Do not stop till the systems reach your expectations.

Look at any sizable organisation. Study any long lasted organisation. You will find robust systems. Longetivity of the organisation is directly proportional to system based working of the organisation. Strong are the systems; longer is the life of organisation. Also, size will grow rapidly if systems are in place.

Systematic working reduces hassles. Systems act like a lubricant, reducing friction. Each individual knows what to do in a particular situation.

In growth times, there is a tendency to bypass systematic working. Short cuts are preferred to complete the task. The enthusiasm to achieve the goals is the major reason for this. However, this enthusiasm may toll a lot in future.

BUILD Q CULTURE

Quality is doing the right thing when no one is looking.
Henry Ford

In late 40's after World War II, Japan as a country, was totally ruined. They chose a path of development thru industrialisation. Initially quantity was their focus. Each Japanese gave his 100%. The quantities were achieved but quality was lost. As a result, Japanese goods were available at reasonable cost but quality was very poor. Customers started discarding Japanese goods.

To overcome the pathetic situation, Japanese Government took help of Dr. Deming, a well known American Guru of Quality Management. He taught Q Culture to Japan industry. The culture is so imbibed in the blood of Japanese, that the stamp "Made in Japan" is treated as a brand. So much, that we do not even bother which company produces it before paying extra premium for the same. Today, Japan is on the top as far as product quality is concerned. It is amongst the richest countries, if per capita income is a criterion.

On the other hand, in today's era, we are experiencing cheap quality goods of China. This is a result of focussing on quantity more than quality. We think ten times before buying goods "Made in China".

This is exactly what happens in growth phase. Quality is compromised for quantity. Cost is used as a tool to grab more business and improve top line. This may help in short term, but in long term, the results are not favourable.

One important point on cost quality relationship; Cost is one time, quality is every time. Offering less cost, can appease the customer one time. But Offering good quality, will please him every time. For a product, cost is paid only once and appreciated or cursed; while quality is experienced each time of usage of product and appreciated or cursed. As quality is discussed much more than cost, it has much more influence than cost.

Quality builds your image. You are watched by every customer on every aspect. In common life, we always use a terminology called "branded product". It is nothing but a synonym of quality. Brands indicate their quality apart from status. We subconsciously presume highest level of perfection while thinking of certain brands. We cannot imagine a Rolex watch showing incorrect time. When it is Mercedes, we are sure on quality and performance. No time we see Toyota cars standing on roadside due to failure of engine.

Quality builds brands. This brand building is not necessarily by spending money. The quality automatically builds the brands attracting customers. See some examples. "Made in Japan", "Made in Swiss", "Made in Germany" are synonymous to engineering excellence. "Made in France" indicates best quality fragrance and wine products. "Produce of Scotland" designate quality of whisky and liqueur. Nobody spent money on building these brands. They are built of their own. It speaks about the quality of product.

Similarly, quality is also associated with the name of a company. If it is Apple iPhone, we know it never hangs. If it is BlackBerry, emails are faster than any other cell phone. If it is a Honda car, it is the best technology. If it is McDonalds, it is the same taste across the world. You will find number of such examples.

Make your quality talk about your organisation. Let the customer say, "If it is XXXX Company, it is defect free."

To define quality in simple words; Quality is what customer wants, stated or unstated. Stated quality is understood easily, unstated needs feedback and analysis. Unstated quality requirements are also equally important. They may not be functionally important but have aesthetic values. Certain gut feels may define the quality. Though these are intangible, it is necessary to identify and fix them.

PROJECT MANAGEMENT

Let our advance worrying become
advance thinking and planning.
Winston Churchill

The major key for growth of an organisation is its Project Management skills. Growth is directly proportional to project management.

The Japanese are considered as the best project management fraternity. They spent 70% of available time on planning and executed the project in remaining 30%. Most of the global industries are adopting a similar strategy.

In project management, rigorous planning is very important. Project management is a specialised job and needs full time attention. As a traditional practice, new projects are handed over to the most efficient blue eyed boy of the organisation. His skill set is not judged on the criterion of project management. Here is the first mistake. Even though this gentleman works at his best, if he does not possess essential skills, he is bound to fail for no fault of his. You lose the project as well as a good person!

There are a number of soft tools available for project planning. These tools are the outcome of lot of brainstorming by experts. Use them. There is no need to reinvent the wheel in the times of F1 Racing...

Further to planning, project monitoring and periodical reviews are utmost important. There are number of tools available.

LEVERAGE YOUR CORE COMPETENCE

Don't invest in a business you don't know.
Warren Buffet

Core competence is an interesting virtue. It is always with you throughout your life. It comes partially from genetic order, somewhat from the personal life, experiences in tender age and balance from your job profile at the start of your career. This has very deep roots in your psyche. When it comes to your core competence, you will always be at your best.

It is always said that convert your hobby into your business. Then you do not work, you just enjoy. To some extent, the same is true about core competence. Working in the core area is always a pleasure. Whatever one knows the best, one gets pleasure doing it. If the subject is close to heart, it is loved.

During growth phase, a point may come when there is a strong desire to diversify. This is of course very good and essential for long term sustainability. For this diversion, the fields chosen are apparently high profitability areas. For ex. engineering industry chooses to enter in real estate or Pharma company opts for share trading, so on and so forth.

Statistically, the failure rate of diversification is very high, if the new area is completely different than core competence. There are respectable exceptions to this; however, this can be taken as a general rule.

There are always good numbers of attractive opportunities available in core competence areas. We should hunt sincerely and whole heartedly. Expanding in core competence gives a back up of confidence. You do not enter into unknown jungle. Every business has tricks of the trade. With your core competence, you already know tricks of your trade. They get deployed horizontally. Every business has a learning cycle. You learnt your business hard way. If you want to learn new competence, it will have its own learning cycle. This consumes time and money. Also, focussing on distinctly different areas is very difficult for a first generation entrepreneur. Even Napoleon lost as he took on different forces at a single time.

Growth is a delicate phase. Here the entrepreneur has come out of starting phase. He has tasted the success. And here is a catch. In growth phase, there is a hazard of this feeling being prominent. Imagine the growth is planned in non core business and one has the feeling that he can't lose.............

This book is for the first generation entrepreneurs. Hence the above deliberation is more applicable mostly to FGEs. They have limited resources. They are just trying to groom with a long way to go. Risk taking is a part and parcel of any business. Smart and calculated risk taking is the key to succeed. Those who have plenty of money, crossed sustenance stage and want to expand can enter in unknown field easily as they have plenty of resources, sustainable organisations and above all, relatively small failures do not affect them. This is not the case with FGEs.

With all this, just look at the big global companies. Take example of Walmart. It is only in retailing and nothing else. McDonalds is only in ready-to-eat fast food, IBM only in hardware and Hershey in chocolates. There are numerous examples to prove that success ratio is very high in core area of operations.

The most recent example of debacle in noncore segment is Kingfisher Airlines in India. It is owned by one of the notable and cash rich industrial house, with a core competence of liquor manufacturing and selling across the globe. Clash in core competence is one of the reasons, amongst many others, for this disaster.

When Mr. Ratan Tata took over as a Chairman of Tata Group, the first thing he did was selling out all noncore businesses. He concentrated on core areas like steel, automotive IT and finance. As a result, Tata Group has grown tenfold during his tenure, standing tall as the largest group in India. (Market cap is more than 100 billion USD. The next follower is Reliance with 62 billion USD, in 2013.)

All such examples underline the importance of core competence for FGE. Why to take undue risk?

TIME MANAGEMENT

A man must be master of his hours and days, not their servant.
William Frederick Book

In the world of Basic Sciences, time is treated as a fourth dimension. It stops passing when the speed is beyond speed of light. But in management, time has different definition and meaning. In management terms, time is a resource, a wonderful resource. It has very peculiar characteristics. Let us see some of them.

1) It is a unidirectional vector. It moves only in forward direction.

2) It is priceless. It cannot be purchased or sold. It does not matter how rich you are, you cannot buy the time.

3) It is the only resource available equally for everyone. Wealthy or deprived, man or woman, boss or subordinate, political or non-political, American or Asian, each own 24 hours in a day and 60 minutes an hour. There is no discrimination.

4) It will never stop functioning. Regardless of whatever happens, it moves on. Earthquake, tsunami, cloud burst, nothing can stop the functioning of time.

Now, just imagine. If all of us have this resource in the same amount, why not everybody can be Bill Gates,

Warren Buffet or Steve Jobs? Is it because they were god gifted? Absolutely not! Read their biographies. All of these three top businessmen on the earth are FGEs! They fought with much more or at least equal hardships than all of us gone through. The main reason of their success is their time management or effective utilisation of time.

The importance of time is beyond doubts. Successful people utilise the time effectively. Napoleon the Great was taking a nap on the galloping horse. This is one of the best examples of time management.

Wasting time gives joy. This joy is temporary. You realise it when the time is gone. The competitors are far ahead of you. Your position in market is descending. Hardly anything is left in hands to correct the situation. Better wake up now and here! Start using your time effectively. Treat time like money. Be a miser! Identify your time stealers. Work on them. Start maintaining a diary. Allocate time to every program in a day. Use DWM (Daily Works Management) tool.

There are number of books on Time Management and DWM (Daily Works Management). Refer them to get scientific details.

In general, main time stealers are:
    a. Television
    b. Checking emails every ten minutes
    c. Continuous checking incoming emails on cell phone.
    d. Excessive use of cell phone.
    e. Games on cell phone / tablet /PC.
    f. No delegation / improper delegation.
    g. Meetings without prior circulation of agenda.

h. Attending meetings without proper homework.
i. No concentration in meetings.
j. Working without DWM
k. Incorrect judgement of traffic / travel time
l. Late reaching on workplace

GROWTH

External

SMELL THE OPPORTUNITY

A wise man will make more opportunities than he finds.
Sir Francis Beckon

FGE has this virtue in his genes. As he can smell the opportunity in external environment, he could start and grow.

As the business grows, one gets entangled more and more in routine. He forgets looking towards outside world. For him, the existing work becomes his world. He enjoys the routine problems and stays happy with his indispensability. This weakens his power of smelling opportunities. Opportunities knock the door and go back if there is no response.

While travelling, if you are watching only your own feet and pamper on the speed, you are bound to lose the foresight. You cannot see the competitors passing by and moving with the pace. Keep your senses awake. Smell, sense, feel, listen and taste it. Grab the right opportunity. It may not give a second chance. Something having the strength to change the ball game may already have gone.

Small chances can change the life. Acceptance of offer to install Windows free of cost on all IBM machines, changed life of Bill Gates.

Opportunities exist in air. Smell them and act upon. Some failed attempts wont matter. Failure is not a crime.

FINANCIAL MANAGEMENT

"Rule number one: Never lose money. Rule number two: Never forget rule 1
Warren Buffet

Statistics shows that 75% FGEs are technocrats. We often come across a remark "He is a hard core technocrat." Just check if following points are associated with this remark:

1. Is he not good at commercials / business.
2. Is he not good at negotiation skills?
3. Is he not good at purchasing skills?

With due regards to respectable exceptions, many technocrat FGEs have finance phobia. This syndrome makes them uncomfortable with financial statements. They always try to get away from commercial issues or try to wind up them at earliest. The quality of decision deteriorates when it comes to mercantile practices.

Any business or organisation revolves around money. One and only one criterion of successful business is its bottom line on financial papers. Anybody related to business, especially in top management, cannot keep himself away from financial affairs. He has to understand commercials. He should possess or learn skills necessary for financial management.

Money in the organisation is never in liquid form. It exists in different places:

1)   In customer's bank accounts

2) In raw material stocks
3) In work in progress
4) In advance taxes paid to Government
5) In scrap
6) In assets
7) Advances to stakeholders
   and so on.

Money at every place has a different characteristic. It will behave differently for same treatment and yield distinct results. For ex. Fixed assets cannot be easily liquidated compared to current assets. Payments blocked with customers for 30 days are simpler to receive than money blocked for 100 days or more. FGE has to be aware of such traits of money at every place to manage the business efficiently.

If not managed properly, money will start showing its typical virtue of evaporation. It evaporates in any direction. If one is not sensitive enough to smell this, it is reflected only in your bank accounts after a long long time. Till the time one realises this, it's too late.

Mastering financial management is the key factor to succeed. Never underestimate it. Focus on the same.

IF YOU WANT ONE,
TRY TWENTY

If you want to increase your success
rate, double your failure rate.
Thomas J. Watson

For every human being, who wants to be an achiever, has to work hard to reach the goal. He has to face number of failures to get one success. Abraham Lincoln won only one election in his lifetime. Thomas Alva Edison failed 1000 times to invent electric bulb.

As a thumb rule, success rate is five percent. Whether this five percent is first five or last five, nobody knows. If it is first five, do not start cheering, start working for next five to come. If it is last five, do not be nervous. Just accelerate your attempts to bring these five percent at earliest.

There are no free lunches. There is no cakewalk. Destiny never helps if you are idle. Luck always favours a brave man.

Go through the biographies of great people. Nobody could succeed overnight. Everyone is gone through rigorous hardship. There were number of challenges, countless adversities and innumerable sacrifices. It is similar to get designated as "Saint". You have to go thru many acid tests.

Swami Vivekananda, an all time great philosopher from India says, "In a day, when you don't come across any problems - you can be sure that you are travelling in a wrong path". Do not get disappointed with problems. Problems are landmark of the destination. Problems indicate that your path is correct.

Remember, five percent success rate means only one attempt out of twenty is successful. If you achieve more, it's your good luck. In any case, you are chosen one by the Almighty. En-cash it as much as you can. You are born to succeed. You have potential to reach to the top.

LEARNING WILL COST

If you think education is expensive, try ignorance.
Derek Bok

During growth phase, you face several issues from external environment. This is a position where you are never before. So you struggle to adjust yourself in new shoes. This is not your comfort zone till date. Naturally, you are uncomfortable in the beginning. You have to learn dealing with these issues.

To achieve the growth, you make various attempts on all fronts. No stone is unturned. As you start achieving the goals, you start facing new challenges. As you want new heights, you have to adopt new ways. You cannot walk the same path and expect different destination. These are the untrodden ways for you. On a new path, one feels nervous initially. There is a tendency to reject.

Here comes the role of learning. We need to learn handling new challenges, experienced never before. Unless we learn and adopt these, our performance will be mediocre.

Such situations are commonly experienced during managing new customers in BtoB scenario. We adopt all marketing tactics to attract a new customer. When new customer actually starts dealing with us, we serve him based on our old practices. We assume the situations and deal with it based on our previous experience with existing customers. We forget to consider the specific needs of new customer. Here the conflict starts.

During growth, there are a lot of new lessons an organisation has to learn. This learning has a cost attached to it. Cost doesn't necessarily mean monetary cost. It is in terms of money, time, energy and personal sacrifices.

Whenever you are entering in growth zone, do not hesitate to spend money on qualitative training. It always helps. Many companies are miser to train the people with a fear of attrition after training. Not to forget, working with trained personnel for short time is much more economical than working with untrained personnel for long time.

While growing, you have to devote more time towards nitty-gritty. Do not assume everything based on your previous experiences. Observe the new scenario. Good observation leads to good analysis. Analyse the situation. Find out what is different than existing. Act upon.

Investment of time is the essential investment to understand new business. Spend it qualitatively and liberally. At times, it is psychologically difficult to come out of routine and concentrate on new business. This cost will be much more. Better invest the maximum available time on new projects. If you want to grow, you should spend 80% of your time on future and 20% on routine. This completes your learning cycle faster.

Needless to mention, unless you have untiring energy with fire in the belly, achievements are difficult. As a cost to succeed, one must build in this energy. Same is the case with personal sacrifices. Success is not free of cost. It demands lots of sacrifices.

PROBLEMS ARE NOT AS SEVERE AS THEY APPEAR

The difference between what we do and what we are capable of doing would suffice to solve most of the world's problem.
Mahatma Gandhi

Problems are not stop signs. They are signals. Every red signal is followed by yellow and green. Every dark night is followed by a beautiful dawn.

Look back in the problems faced by you in your life. Every time you came out with flying colours. Isn't it? Your son was not well, had high fever and you were worried. You had a catfight with your sister and decided not to see her face. Your boss blasted on you yesterday and you were worried on promotion. Your customer found rejected pieces in the supplies and was very upset. Every time you were thinking about the worst possibilities. You expected disasters. In reality, none of the disaster crossed your way. Something might have gone wrong momentarily, but was it a disaster? Did you not handle the situation with courage and succeed to overcome?

This is what happens every time. Your own mind is the biggest devil. It will always put forward negative things first. It will stretch the imagination till the worst possible. A small business switch in favour of your competitor gives a feeling of end of the world. Some financial loss results into dizziness.

Success of counterpart increases palpitation. Delay in project execution leads to hypertension. Competitor's progress pilots stomach-ache. Even best friend's foot forward navigates heart-aches. We treat them as severe problems in our life. Are they really severe?

Avoiding the problem increases gravity of the problem. Face it immediately. Face bigger problems first! Do not waste time. Just as you are scared of the problem, problems are also scared of you. They will run away as soon as you confront them.

In some cases, our real problem is we do not know what we want to achieve. We want to do everything and end up being jack of all than master of one. We do not plan our own activities to grow and just try to copy others. A copy is never as good as original. This causes collapse, subsequently frustration and then depression. If we define our goals clearly, our 80% problems will vanish then and there. Try this!

Out of balance 20%, more than 15% problems come with solutions, hand in hand. The problem itself will lead to solutions. For ex. Competitor grabs a business in bidding. You also know the business equally well. You can easily find out the reasons for going orders to the competitor. Analyse his strengths and your weaknesses and try to get same or next order.

To take another example, say there is IR issue and workers union is reacting. Instead of reacting harsh, go to the root of the issue, sit across the table, discuss, convince or get convinced and try to resolve the issue for long term. If there is undue and illogical demand from other end, there is no choice than taking tough stand. Is there any third scenario possible? The problem has come with the solution.

In remaining 5%, more than 4% problems are resolved with little extra efforts, not done before. Say, raising own capital for growth. As all funds are blocked in current business, it is difficult to raise own capital. Such issues are to be dealt individually and on case to case basis.

The last 1% may be the real issues. Many times these are related to external environment and we hardly have any control on such issues. For ex. Fluctuation in dollar rate, change in economic policy of the country, new legislation passed in parliament, opposition party coming in power, force measure or act of God etc. Such problems are beyond our capacity and we can hardly influence them. Best way is to accept them and find the solution best suited for our organisation.

To summarise, problems are not as severe as they appear. Every problem is faced by us or someone else at some point of time. It has a standard solution. Sit down and think! 99% problems are not the problems and on balance 1% you do not have any control! Why to worry?

SUSTENANCE

—∞∞∞—

Personal

FINANCIAL DISCIPLINE

Sustenance phase is the most critical of all three phases. It has challenges different from start and growth phase. We discussed on financial management in growth phase. Financial discipline is indeed a part of financial management. However, in sustenance phase, financial discipline should be exclusively focussed.

Broadly, financial discipline is to be focussed on following points:

1) Allocate the funds properly:
   Proper planning and correct thought process solves your 90% issues. Plan to the last penny. Follow monthly and annual budgeting procedure rigorously. Do periodical reviews. Analyse variances. Make action plans to correct them.

2) Use the funds only for allocated purpose:
   Use long term debts for long term applications like land, building, plant and machinery. Similarly, use short term loans for short term applications like working capital. It is a normal tendency to use short term loans for long term applications. This affects your financial papers adversely.

3) Do not siphon the funds:
Draining out funds from the business is always detrimental. Once the balance is lost, it is difficult to straighten the situation.

4) Do not divert the funds for other business:
Raise different funds for other business. Diversion is equally detrimental as siphoning.

5) You are a trustee of your bank account:
There are number of stakeholders in the money you possess in your bank account. You are only the trustee of that sum. Spend it wisely.

CREATIVITY

"Imagination is everything. It is the preview of life's coming attractions."
Albert Einstein

Creativity is also deliberated in Personal issues during Start phase. Specifically, the same topic is applicable in Sustenance phase, with different context.

Starting and growing is a long journey. It is tiresome. It is painful. It calls for numerous sacrifices. To gain something, you lose a lot. The most important thing you lose is your creativity. It is the first and foremost victim.

Remember your childhood and adolescence. Recollect the ideas you were creating and enjoying on their implementation. It may not yield you handsome money, but it surely was giving you a great pleasure.

The whole reason to reiterate "Creativity" is because in this distant travel, you tend to forget it. The pressure of performance and achievement victimise creativity. It is the asset with which you started your journey. Preserve it! Use it as far as possible. Creativity attracts more creativity. It is in your blood. Just rejuvenate it every time.

DELEGATION PHASE 2

"Never tell people how to do things. Tell them what to do and they will surprise you with their ingenuity."
General George Smith Patton, Jr.

Delegation is discussed in start phase of business. There it is coming as an internal issue of the organisation. This is for a simple reason that organisation is facing different challenges in this phase. The people in the organisation are new to each other. Working as a team is an important aspect in this phase. Delegation plays a pivotal role in team building. In the organisation, every boss should start trusting in his subordinate. Trust is reflected thru delegation. Everyone in the organisation should work in the same direction to achieve the goals set. Delegation in Phase 1, inside the organisation helps bringing everyone closer to form a group with synergy. Hence Delegation Phase 1, during start of business is an Internal Issue.

Delegation Phase 2 is a personal issue of FGE. In the starting phase, there are limitations on certain delegations. As everyone is new with the organisation, entrepreneur is testing the waters. The first and foremost requirement of delegation is trust. For certain sensitive areas, trust building takes some time. Hence there are limitations on delegation in the areas like finance, accounting, customer relationship management, IR, etc. in spite of strong will and wish, FGE could not delegate certain authorities. This is because subordinates may have some limitation; or FGE has not understood the subordinates fully. Also, there is lack of experience of subordinates. The potential is not fully explored. Above all, FGE is also inexperienced and always try to play safe.

In the phase of sustenance, individual FGE has a big role to play. If he is entangled in routine work, he cannot look forward. Only those companies succeed, grow and sustain, whose CEOs eventually become USELESS for routine work!

Conventionally, 80:20 principle states that you should spend 80% of your time for future and 20% for routine. Practically, higher is the ratio, better it is! The most ideal ratio is 99:1. Warrant Buffet, Guru of Gurus, holds more than 50 companies in his basket. He writes only one letter to each CEO, every year. The letter gives his comments on performance of past year, targets for next year and plans for coming five years. This is the only time he spends on each company.

To make the organisation sustainable and take it to the next level, it is important that the big boss is free from routine. He should get quality time to think. With all said and done, however high EQ one possess, the brain cannot be switched on and off like an electric bulb. It takes time to get a link of thoughts. We need to spend a quality time to think.

The sensitive areas mentioned above are normally kept close to heart. Delegation of these areas is thought of ten times before execution. That is right! You need trusted soldiers for this.

Till you reach to the phase of sustenance, organisation is well developed. You have developed the people and aligned them for organisational goals. You have alternatives available. Find out competent people with right skill set for sensitive areas and delegate! Do not wait! Take some risks. Even identify if someone can sign cheques / bills on your behalf. Let your CFO deal with your bankers and permit your Marketing Manager to close the deals directly with the customer.

The Big Boss should be invisible like God. He need not be present physically, but his presence should be felt. It is felt thru targets, reviews, monitoring, helping at proper stuck ups etc. If he is visible and seen physically everywhere, solves all problems, then he acts as if he works under everyone, (a peon???????).

LEARN MANAGING PROFITS

When forced to choose, I will not trade even a
night's sleep for the chance of extra profits."
Warren Buffet

An entrepreneur cannot reach a phase of sustenance unless he makes profits in growth phase. Business is meant for profits. If there is no profit, it is not a business. When profits start generating, entrepreneur starts enjoying the business. He starts understanding the tricks of trade. He is enthused. Motivation levels increase. More efforts are put in. This generates more money.

Entrepreneur has handled money since starting phase. Every penny is specified to a fixed cause. Initial capital is utilised for fixed assets. After starting of actual sales, the funds are allocated for working capital. In growth phase, additional funds are assigned for new plant and machinery, so on and on. The important thing to note is, every penny is spent on a fixed purpose.

Profit is surplus money. It is the money which is generated by your business and does not have immediate allocation. It is spare money in the system.

One has to be cautious in this mode. This is a dicey situation. When you do not have money, you always want to have it. As soon as you get money, you are confused! The first confusion is what to do with this money? Generally, FGE does not have very high personal requirements. Very few of them have glorious and glamorous lifestyles. Piling up money in the bank account leads to perplexing.

Money is a difficult commodity to handle. If you do not possess it, you are depressed. This is obvious. But if you have it and cannot use it, it is more depressing. This depression makes you desperate. This desperation compels you to undertake some new venture. Apparently, this can be high profit making, but may not be your core competence. Here you are dependent on someone who knows the new business. You solely trust him and one fine morning, you realise the reality, that New venture is in terrific state of affair! Then you consol yourself using a term "Business Risk" and write off the losses.

Just think! Why someone else will work to make you rich? He will have his own interests and hidden agendas. Dependence on others will never yield fruits. There are neither free lunches nor easy money. If you are investing based on someone else's competence, be careful!

No one on this earth makes a charity while doing business. Business is business and charity is charity. Bill Gates gives majority of his earning to Bill and Melinda Charitable Trust. But Microsoft does not reduce its margin of profit. Microsoft earns its pie ruthlessly. In turn this profit may go back to society, but only thru the Bill and Melinda Charitable Trust and not from Microsoft business.

Profit Management is a subject of its kind. This is to be handled carefully. Money is highly volatile. It is to be constantly distilled to convert in liquid state. In liquid state, it has properties of mercury. It flows easily in any direction and does not keep any traces of existence while going to other place. It is to be handled very carefully and delicately.

Profit is secured only if it is reinvested correctly. Reinvestment is highest secured when you are in total command of the investment. Find out the areas of your total command.

Is this Total Command area your own business? Have you reached this stage because this is now your core competence? Do you know your business inside out? Is return on investment fairly good?

If the answers are affirmative, consider ploughing back profits in your own business. Find opportunities of attracting more business by adding new equipments. Try making additional profits using new technologies. Improve quality standards with automation. There can be many options.

This may not be the only solution managing profits. But surely this is the safest way to manage the profits correctly, till you become a giant and sustainable organisation.

EMOTIONAL DETACHMENT

Always perform your duty efficiently and without attachment to the results, because by doing work without attachment one attains the Supreme.
Bhagavad Gita

We discussed "Emotional Attachment" in starting phase, as a personal issue. Exactly contrary is "Emotional Detachment" as a personal issue in sustenance phase. This detachment is only with reference to organisation and not with reference to people in the organisation. In the beginning, emotional attachment is must, as it brings in passion. Passion is the foundation for success.

As the organisation grows, passion grows. This leads to achievements. Achievements strengthen the emotional bonds. This is necessary even in growth phase.

If the same level of emotional attachment is continued in sustenance phase, it gets converted in possessiveness. Possessiveness enjoys concentration of power and decision making. This reduces delegation which is a mandatory phase for sustenance.

Sustenance of any organisation depends on TEI, i.e. Total Employee Involvement. Unless the top boss is detached emotionally, involvement of subordinates is not possible. Emotional involvement leads to undue interference in the system. If boss is taking or influencing all decisions, subordinates cannot grow to their fullest potential. They will remain mediocre.

Hence, the boss should not be possessive of authority. He should be emotionally detached from the routine and maximise delegation. In the best organisation, absence of boss does not affect the overall performance. It is equally good in his presence or absence.

For some bosses, emotional detachment may give a feeling of insecurity. They shiver with a thought of subordinate surpassing them. Such bosses are not confident about themselves. They are reached to their maximum potential. If they continue to think the same, there position is stagnant. They do not realise that unless they make someone capable of replacing them, they cannot move up the ladder. Those who get detached emotionally, make themselves free. They start earning more time. This time they utilise for their own uplift, in turn taking the organisation to next level.

Further, there is a high probability that a subordinate can do a typical job much better than his boss. Explore those possibilities.

There is a simple test to identify an emotionally attached boss. This is applicable in sustenance phase and not in start or growth phase. Just observe his behaviour after office hours. If he is talking only about the organisation, customers and his superiors after office hours, weekly offs and holidays, he is an emotionally attached boss. In long run, there will be certain limitations on his career. He is scared of his performance. He is worried of the competition he has to face.

There is no harm in talking about job and superiors after office hours. However, it should not take control of your life. You should be in commanding position of your destiny.

Also one can easily identify emotionally detached boss. He will take regular reviews. The reviews will be hard and rigorous. However, once reviews are over, he will not discuss about it till the next review. He will attend informal get-togethers but will not utter a single word on official matters. He knows the personal life of his subordinate and subordinate goes to him for advice on personal issues.

Emotional detachment with organisation gives you more time to connect with people in the organisation. Invest more time in people. For the boss, it will yield much better results than investing time on physically working.

SUSTENANCE

—⧈—

Internal

LOYAL WORKFORCE

You never have to chase people down and beg for their loyalty and respect. It's either they're with you or they're not.

Organisation is people. Whatever automation you do and systems you install, the brain behind machines and structure is important.

Loyalty is an essential parameter. This imitates intangibly. Longevity of association is surely one of the indicators but may not be the only one.

Only loyal workforce will raise the organisation to higher altitude. Smooth running of organisation depends on loyalty of the people working in the organisation. Floating workforce does not add great value to the system. That is the reason nowadays, psychometric tests are gaining importance. These tests will tell clearly if the individual can gel with the organisation, considering his traits and behavioural pattern.

There are certain quick tests to understand the loyalty of any individual with the boss and the organisation:

- ➢ Casual, sick and earned leaves are prior / timely intimated and planned.
- ➢ Mostly, leaves do not adjoin weekly off.
- ➢ Cell phones are picked before ringing of third bell.

- ➢ Heated exchanges are taken in right spirit.
- ➢ Employee does not hesitate to spat with superiors for right cause.
- ➢ Avoids gossiping about company matters.
- ➢ Develops his own review mechanism.
- ➢ Every day, while going home after office hours, he/she is not stressed out.
- ➢ Does not stare the wrist watch after office hours.
- ➢ Frequently uses the word "We" in the conversation.

As a general rule, loyal people stay with the organisation for substantially longer period. If cared properly on emotional and economic front, such people can devote whole life with the organisation.

A great American Film producer famously said, "I'll take fifty percent efficiency to get one hundred percent loyalty." It is possible that sometimes, few loyalists may be average performers. Still they prove to be much better than unfaithful high performers. The best example is Judas identified by Christ in last supper.

Loyal workforce is gathered over a period. One needs to work from day one to build loyalty in people. Subordinates always treat the boss as their idol. They watch every move and derive their own inferences out of it. All acts, whether good or bad, are correlated by them in their own context. The loyalty starts when faith is built in the people. Everyone needs security. This security comes from three E's: Emotional, Economical and Environmental.

Emotional security is about wavelength matching and personal bonding. It is important the thought process matches with that of the organisation. Loyalty will follow. Also, when someone is liked on individual level, the ties become stronger.

Environment in the organisation has more impact than emotions on a loyalist. Everyone expects to build his career. Everybody loves working with continually growing organisation. Each individual wants new challenges. If the working environment does not fulfil this need, loyalty shakes.

Every one works for money. Period! For a common man, the first and foremost need is money. Money is a strong magnet. Of course, it has only 1/3rd impact on the loyalty. If other two E's are right, outside E, i.e. Economy cannot pull out a loyalist.

In long run, loyalty of your employee will earn you its royalty.

MOTIVATION

Motivation is either internal or external. Internal is from within, external is from fear of extinction.

In the science of management, motivation is a buzz word. Refer any management book and you will find various theories on motivation and different techniques to motivate people. Many management gurus have done a lot of researches on motivation and there are numerous examples of how motivation turned around the organisation which were on the verge of collapsing. I found some shocking outcomes of motivation in my working life.

Motivation exists in two forms only:
1) Internal motivation
2) Motivation through fear

I could not find a third type of motivation during my whole working life till now. Now, I am a firm believer that external motivation has temporary impact. It does not last long.

People, who are internally motivated, do not need any reward for their performances. Whether awarded or not, they still continue to perform. Success does not seduce them and failure does not demoralise them. More than the results, they believe in efforts. They are not worried for calamities. They demonstrate high energy levels and are always enthusiastic. This is the best form of motivation.

One of the best examples for companies obsessed with internally motivated people is 3M. They own a huge number of patents. See the amazing product portfolio of innovative products. Du Pont or Corning is the similar company with internally motivated people. Watch their performances. It is mind blowing! Such companies have a very long life cycle. They cannot perish. They get matured and stronger with time.

The other type is motivation through fear. The word fear does not mean frightening. It simply indicates that if someone is not internally motivated, he will not perform unless he has a fear for his survival in the organisation.

This technique is successfully used by number of stalwarts. Jack Welch took over when General Electric Company was not doing well. He linked everything with performance. Perform or perish was the punch line. The condition of GE was weak. There was a chaos. This Electric Giant Company was sleeping and Jack had a mammoth task to awake the giant and make it dance to rhythm. As non performers started disappearing, a fear started working. Everyone pulled up their socks. Brains got activated and hands started working. People were aligned. Targets were visible. All tug of wars ended and unidirectional efforts started showing colours.

In Big4 consultancy firms, the rule is, seek promotion in three years, based on KRA achievements or get out. The fear of losing keeps everyone on toes and organisation starts performing.

One of an interesting case study of motivation thru fear is Japan, as country. In World War II, Japan was completely collapsed. There was a real fear for survival of mankind in the country. Every one stood united. The fear worked positively. Whole country was aligned. Today it is the richest economy in the world.

On the other hand, USA is a country of internally motivated people. Most of the citizens of USA are not real natives. They are migrated in search of opportunities. All are internally motivated to perform in land of opportunities. That is another richest country in the world.

TRAINING

One of the neglected areas in most organisations is training. In difficult times, first budget cut is axed on training. It is considered as a non value adding activity. This is far away from reality. It is always better to work with trained personnel. People need maintenance and upgrades even more than machines do. Retraining is maintenance. Training is an upgrade. Development is the next generation model.

Apart from clearing the concepts, training helps in alignment of ground staff with top management. Human beings are crazy for recognition. Each of us wants an identity. One is prepared to exert for the same. The problem is to identify the target and find a way to reach the target.

Training is the best media to explain the targets and teach the ways to achieve the same. Right training will make the task easier.

What is important before training is to identify the training needs. Each individual has some expertise. Training in the same will improve the skills. However, there are areas which are unknown. Training in such areas will help him grow. Identify the needs and work on it. Training has a power to transform companies. Mahindra and Mahindra, a company known only for small SUVs and tractors, tied up with Indian Institute of Management. In a limited span, the transformation is delighting. Today it is successfully operating from two wheelers to aeroplane. Apart from automotive, it is into IT, Engineering and R&D. The major contributor in this transformation is training.

Be careful in identifying the needs. This should support the vision of management. Equally important is the choice of trainer. Trainer should be aware of necessities of the organisation. He should understand the culture and design his course accordingly.

STRONG REVIEW MECHANISM

<u>"What's measured improves"</u>
<u>Peter F. Drucker</u>

We had seen importance of delegation. However, only delegation does not solve the purpose. Rather, situation will be more complex if delegation is not followed by periodical reviews. Delegation needs monitoring. Structured monitoring enhances the impact of delegation. Building strong review mechanism is the key for structured monitoring.

In any organisation, smooth flow of information is utmost necessary. If the information flows at all levels, there is a clarity on direction of progress. This brings unity in the organisation.

Design of review mechanism should be customised. The period of review is directly related to organisation chart. As a thumb rule, higher is the level, larger is the period of review. Maximum period of review should not exceed one month.

Reviews are of three types:
1) Routine review
2) Project review
3) Emergency review
1) Routine review: Routine reviews are done more frequently. They are of various types as follows:

a) Operational review: Shop floor and sales activities are to be reviewed daily. Around 98% review points are common. Prepare a checklist and go through it every morning. Start of the day should be with this review. Normal points are related to operations yesterday, today and tomorrow. This review should be in small related groups such as production cell 1, production cell 2, maintenance cell, stores cell etc. etc. there will be various meetings happening simultaneously. Maximum duration of this meeting should be 10 minutes. These meetings will not yield results held for more than 10 minutes and there is no checklist present. Immediately after this meeting, heads of each cell meet with plant in charge for 10 minutes to discuss yesterday, today and tomorrow.

b) Financial review: Period for this review is one month. It is important to check the financial position of the company every month. FGE mostly being a technocrat tends to avoid this and faces surprise at the end of the year. There should be rigorous reviews along with all the key people. To improve the performance, accountability is to be improved and if you want the people to be accountable, they should be aware of financial health and measures needed to improve the same. They add great value to financial strength of the company.

c) Performance review: In most of the organisations, annual package revisions are done based on annual performance review. Actually, this will yield high returns if the frequency is three months. A well structured performance review, backed up with written KRAs will give best results.

2) Project review: There are number of projects going on simultaneously in any organisation. They are categorised as
   i) Internal : Related to routine operations
   ii) External : Related to new development
   The frequency varies on case to case basis. Maximum frequency should not exceed beyond a month.

3) Emergency review: To resolve unforeseen issues creating emergency situation, emergency reviews are organised. They are normally with a single point agenda and stretched in single sitting till the issue is resolved.

For all reviews except emergency review, a standardised format should be designed. This makes the meetings meaningful, focussed and saves on time. Remember, smaller meetings are more productive.

DAILY WORKS MANAGEMENT

"The bad news is time flies. The good news is you're the pilot."
Michael Altshuler

DWM or Daily Works Management is a simple technique to save your time and energy. In turn, it reduces undue work pressures. It helps streamlining tasks, remembering issues and managing available time effectively.

One can use his own format for DWM. An easy method to prepare a good format is as follows:

a) Enlist all activities you need to do and you remember at this point of time.

b) Mention the frequency with which you perform these activities.

c) Bifurcate all activities as per frequency, i.e., daily, alternate day, weekly, fortnightly, monthly, quarterly, half yearly and yearly.

d) Mention the time in minutes, you need for each activity.

e) Take a calendar and fill above information for the month, quarter and year. This is very easy if you use electronic calendar. It will take maximum one hour to fill the electronic calendar for a complete year.

Making DWM chart for a year takes only 2-3 hours. Once you prepare it, you will find that you have the workload of only 20% of total time available with you. Now you have 80% of time with you to take more loads and reach new heights.

ASSERT

Don't say YES when you want to say NO
Herbert Fensterheim & Jean Baer

In starting phase, we elaborated on humbleness of the FGE. This humbleness helps him to learn new things. Facing unknown with humility always helps. After passing this phase and enriched with experience, FGE reaches the phase of sustenance. With all other virtue, organisation should also learn assertion. Assertion is not antonym of humble. It is complementary.

To please the boss or customer, one takes humbleness to the level of goodie goodie talk. He enters "Yes Sir" category and becomes "Yes Man". This leads to accept undesired tasks resulting in series of failures.

Customer or boss does not necessarily appreciate Yes Man. May be they appreciate at that moment, but will never stand by you in case of failure on same point. Temporary solutions become permanent problems. Praise for a moment leads to abuses for long.

To sustain the business, assertion at proper time helps a lot. Some time, you may come one step backward. Look at sprint runners. To go forward rapidly, one step backward will help.

SUSTENANCE

—————— ∞∞ ——————

External

WIDEN SECTOR BASE

"Without continual growth and progress, such words as improvement, achievement, and success have no meaning"
Benjamin Franklin

With growth and sustenance, much is talked about widening customer base to make the organisation strong. Certainly this is essential. Widening the customer base reduces over dependency. This mellows down the direct impact of variation in customer performance. As we are aware, customer requirement directly affects our results. If the year is good for the customer, we are in good shape and reverse is also true.

Having broader customer portfolio reduces this problem to a great extent. Poor orders from one customer get compensated by good orders from other. Performance near the average line on annual basis is more predictable and surely better if customer portfolio is good.

It is equally significant to have the total revenue coming in from different customers, be nearly similar in terms of percentage. High dependence on single customer may be detrimental for sustaining the business on long term.

Only broadening customer base and earning equalised revenue from all customers may not suffice the purpose. Something going wrong on generic business across the sector will affect it severely. When digital camera was invented, conventional camera industry started vanishing. Kodak, a global company enjoying monopoly, practically disappeared. Today, high megapixel mobile phones are replacing digital cameras. In next few years (months??) digital camera industry may start counting its days.

Hence, apart from increasing customer base, one must think of widening sector base also. The skills acquired could also be utilised effectively in some other sectors. Try to conquer that sector. This will make the business shockproof.

Recession is a periodic phenomenon. It will repeat with a typical frequency. When recession starts, the first affected sectors are real estate and automotive. The companies depending only on either of the sector pass through tough time. Instead, if the dependence is divided sector wise, probability of down turn reduces.

CONSOLIDATION

Consolidation is the first step before long leap.

Consolidation is the key of sustenance. During growth, many decisions are taken hurriedly. Often the depth of thinking at that point is less. Also, with experience, you gained additional knowledge and can use it to improve overall performance.

Planned growth has limitations. If you want to grow, you should catch hold of opportunities. Opportunities do not come with pre-intimation. Very often they knock the door when you are ill-equipped. Many times, situation calls for on the spot decisions. This is the necessity of any business.

The side effect of growth is development of inefficiency in the organisation. As you start entering in sustenance phase, take a pause. Look inside the organisation. Scan complete organisation meticulously. Find out areas for improvement. Identify loopholes.

After Enlisting above issues, form a task force. Make an action plan for consolidation. Decide stretched targets. Assign the responsibilities. Review periodically to achieve the goals.

Consolidation has many advantages. Apart from bringing efficiency in the organisation, it recharges the organisation. It may vacate the space and spare some machines. This is as good as adding resources, free of cost!

Watch the transformation phases of big companies. The first thing any top management does is consolidation. The great persona of Indian industry, Hon'ble. Mr. Ratan Tata, when occupied the office, did consolidation as the very first thing. He decided the core areas and sold out other businesses. In his regime, Tata Group grown multi fold and today it is undisputed leader of Indian industry.

In his second inning, Mr. NR Narayanmurthy, founder Chairman of Infosys, adopted the same technique. To improve the performance of Infosys, he chopped all noncore businesses, streamlined all verticals to consolidate and succeed.

Consolidation is a periodic process. It needs to be done with a specified frequency. Business is always dynamic. Lot of things are continuously changing. Before moving ahead, look back and contemplate. This gives energy for next sprint, to win the race.

ANTICIPATE THE COMPETITION

Jealousy is love in competition
Toba Beta

Competition is inevitable. It exists from pin to piano. Monopoly virtually does not exist. As soon as some business starts earning good profits, competition appears. And it is much tougher than you expect.

Visualising the competition is ok! But it may be too late. When you visualise something, it is very near. If you visualise the competition, it is sure that the same is in your doorstep. Hence, do not visualise, anticipate!

Competition is ruthless! It is always cut throat. No one spares you. It follows jungle law or Darwin theory. Fittest will survive!

Keep your antennas open. If you want to sustain, keep an eye on the external environment. Be a crow, looking at two directions at a time. Follow the owl for night vision. Be cautious. Be informed. Analyse the information. Relate it to your business. Think of the worst. Anticipate the probable competition. Keep your plans ready.

Competition is good. It teaches you about this pragmatic world. It keeps you on toes. It makes you think. Performance is always best under pressure.

Look the revolution of automotive industry in India. Till 90's, there was a "Licence Regime" and lot of restrictions on automotive industries. Especially, it was difficult for foreign companies to start manufacturing in India. This killed the competition. Existing automotive manufacturers were enjoying monopoly. As the goods were sold and there was a long waiting list, product quality was below average. After economy opened up in 90's, foreign competition started coming in. There was threat to existing manufacturers. They started improving. Today many Indian automotive manufacturers have their own R&D set ups. Completely Indian origin vehicles are now built with a quality at par with European / American / Japanese standard.

So, anticipate the competition, act up on it and upgrade your organisation. This is one of the best strategy to sustain for long run.

NETWORKING

"If you want to go somewhere, it is best to find
someone who has already been there."
Robert Kiyosaki

During start and growth, networking is in auto mode. One could not start and grow without networking. But this networking is need based and not designed. You do networking as it comes. Here necessity becomes the mother of invention.

In the phase of sustenance, one should design networking. Networking is an essential part of marketing your organisation. Without networking, your real potential may remain to yourself. One cannot expect business without merits. It is important to possess skills and have merits. It is also equally important that others should know your skills and merits. This happens with networking.

Networking is a job of a specialist. It needs a different skill set. Networking backed up by quality and meritorious organisation can conquer the peaks.

BETTER TO HAVE
MORE TROUBLES!

*The real man smiles in trouble, gathers strength
from distress, and grows brave by reflection.*
Thomas Paine

While travelling up to sustenance phase, one has faced numerous troubles. Naturally, no one wants troubles. One and all hate it. We want everything hassle free.

What is the reality? External environment is full of difficulties. You overcome one and another is ready. Every step you will find one.

How to counter this situation?

Go through the biographies of great people. Dhirubhai Ambani, founder of Reliance Group, India, faced huge financial problems from beginning. He countered each one and culture of investing in stock market started in India. He faced numerous health issues but also had a strong will power to overcome the same.

We all know the story of Steve Jobs. His struggle was with his destiny. Troubles were chasing him on personal level, family front, work place and health ground. Hats off to the individual, who created Apple Empire, in spite of troubles on every count.

Ten years back, who thought about Barack Obama being a President of world's most powerful country?

Dr. Deming was not accepted as a consultant by his own country, USA. He went to Japan and today Deming Award, world's most prestigious industrial award is named after him.

Above cases clearly indicate that troubles will follow only those who have ambitions. If you have more ambitions, you will have more troubles. In short, more troubles indicate you have high potential to reach new heights.

Troubles are navigators. They show the directions. A little more courage takes you to next level. Make friendship with them. Face them with a smile. They will show you the way!